TEDDY**BOY**

TEDDY MCCARTHY
with DONAL KEENAN

IRISH SPORTS PUBLISHING

Published by Irish Sports Publishing (ISP)
Unit 11, Tandy's Lane
Lucan, Co Dublin
Ireland
www.irishsportspublishing.com

First published, 2012

A CIP record for this book is available from the British Library

ISBN 978-0-9573954-3-5

Printed in Ireland with Print Procedure Ltd
Cover design, typesetting and layout: Jessica Maile
Photographs: Inpho Sports Agency

DEDICATION

To Oonagh, Cian, Niall and Sinead.

In memory of my father and mother, and my
brother Michael.

CONTENTS

ACKNOWLEDGMENTS

All of my life I have lived in Glanmire. The place and its people have defined me. I was born with a God-given talent and that has allowed me to travel to every corner of Ireland and around the world. It has been a privilege, and for that I am grateful.

It is impossible to compile a list of those people who have accompanied me on my various travels through the life described in the following pages. The list would be too long and I am afraid that I might leave someone out.

I have been lucky in many ways. From my earliest days there were always people looking after me. They were there on the hurling and football fields, in the schools I attended, at work and, most of all, in the home. To all of those people – family members, friends, teachers, coaches at various levels and teammates – I want to record a heartfelt thanks. They know who they are and I hope, in telling my life story, that I do them justice.

It hasn't always been the easiest journey, but my family has always been steadfast in its support. I was the lucky one to be out there on the playing fields enjoying incredible success, but every triumph was shared with the people closest to me because they played an important part. Without them it would never have happened.

What follows is not all about success. There has been tragedy and turbulence along the way, as well. I hope this book serves as a tribute to the resilience of the people around me and as an acknowledgement of how they inspired me and supported me through bad times and good.

Teddy McCarthy, October 2012.

ABOUT THE CO-AUTHOR

Donal Keenan has been one of Ireland's leading sports journalists for the past three decades. He has worked as GAA Correspondent for some of Ireland's major daily and Sunday newspapers, including the *Irish Independent*, *The Sunday Times* and *Ireland on Sunday*. He has also written on some of the major sports events of the world, including the Ryder Cup, the 2002 World Cup in Japan and Korea, as well as major International rugby fixtures throughout Europe.

He first encountered Teddy McCarthy as a minor footballer with Cork in 1983 and followed his career closely thereafter, reporting on all his major triumphs on football and hurling fields. They toured Australia together in 1986 with Kevin Heffernan's ground-breaking Ireland team, and also travelled to the United States. A native of Roscommon now living in Dublin, Donal is the author of a number of books on Gaelic Games.

CHAPTER 1

The final whistle shrilled. I stood alone.

The All-Ireland senior football final of 1990 had just concluded. We had beaten our greatest rivals of the era, Meath. We had many battles during those years that were described as bloody and bitter. This was not one of them.

I shook hands with a couple of Meath players who were standing close to me. Then I embraced my regular midfield partner, Shea Fahy. He had played a fantastic game. I told him that, just before our supporters broke through whatever feeble security cordon had been thrown together to keep them in the stands and on the terraces.

Over the next few minutes, I took more belts than I had throughout the entire Championship. I felt none of them. Complete strangers hugged me. A few kissed me. At one stage I thought I would be smothered. I wriggled free.

With all this euphoria around me, I felt strange. Not subdued. Maybe calm. Possibly relieved. I was still the centre of attention but the pressure had been lifted. My emotions, which had been in a state of turmoil throughout the summer months, returned to something close to normality.

In the mayhem I tried to put my thoughts together. History had just been made and I was central to that. Cork had become the first county to win the All-Ireland senior football and hurling Championships in the same season, and I was the only player to feature on both teams.

My old pal, Denis Walsh, had played on the hurling team but had not been able to secure his place on the football team. He deserved enormous credit for his achievement but the spotlight had focussed on me because I played in both finals. For the previous five years that spotlight had burned down on me. I never got comfortable under its glare, and it would be brighter than ever now.

There was a list of famous players who had won All-Ireland medals in both games and most of them were heroes of mine. Those lists had been reproduced so often in the four weeks before the football final that I knew the names off by heart – Jack Lynch, Jimmy Barry Murphy, Ray Cummins, Brian Murphy... My own name would now be added to that list with the unique distinction of winning medals in the same year.

Two weeks before, the Cork hurlers had staged a dramatic recovery against Galway to win the All-Ireland hurling final. It had been a tense, exciting game. There were stages during the game when we thought it was lost; when maybe it should have been lost if Galway had completed the job.

At the final whistle we celebrated wildly. We were lifted into the air by the supporters and carried to the presentation area at the Hogan Stand. I stood half-way up the steps of the stand and watched as my old pal from schooldays in North Monastery, Tomas Mulcahy, lifted the Liam MacCarthy Cup into the air. It was my second hurling success and I think I appreciated this one more. The first one, in 1986, happened so quickly and in such peculiar circumstances, that will be explained later, that it almost passed me by.

I joined in the celebrations with the hurlers and had a few drinks, but I kept it sensible and under control. Billy Morgan, our football coach, knew he had nothing to worry about when he saw me back in training. The first night back I worked harder than anyone, to prove a point.

Another major event occurred in my life during that fortnight that escaped the attention of everyone except those closest to me. Oonagh, my partner, gave birth to our first child, Cian, who was born on September 9. At the time, it was all part of the roller-coaster that was the life of Teddy McCarthy. In hindsight, I think the birth put everything into perspective.

In the build-up to the football final there was a lot of attention on my role in the game and my potential place in history. It was real pressure. Billy did his best to ease some of that pressure by deflecting attention in whatever way he could.

The media was a smaller grouping then, too. I knew most of the main GAA journalists anyway, having toured abroad with them to Australia and the United States. I gave them as much of my time as they wanted and they left me alone after that. In the days immediately before the game I was kept under wraps. Still, the pressure of the event and the added significance of my possible achievement did weigh heavily.

When it was all over and the supporters descended on the team, I felt a need to be alone. I don't think it was just for myself. I thought about the other players. I'd had my moment two weeks beforehand and I didn't want my presence to distract from what my teammates had just done.

These guys were my friends and they had soldiered hard over the years for everything they had achieved. And they had achieved a great deal, more than any other bunch of Cork footballers had ever achieved in history. They deserved their glory and I would not allow anything to affect that. I decided, there and then, to head for the dressing room.

Most attention was now focused on the Hogan Stand. The stewards and Gardai had formed a cordon and the players found refuge within. I dodged a few embraces and began to make my way towards the corner between the Hogan Stand and the Canal End. A few supporters spotted me but left me alone. I heard a few people shout from the stand but I did not look up.

The steward at the gate to the dressing-room area was surprised to see me coming. "Are you not going up for the presentation, Teddy?" he asked.

"I'll be back out in a minute," I told him. I had no intention of coming back out but I did not expect the surprise that lay in store.

Expecting to be alone, I momentarily was taken aback when I noticed someone else in the dressing room. "Who the hell...?" The thought ended abruptly.

One of my all-time heroes ... Jack Lynch.

The former Taoiseach, the Cork GAA legend, stood there, pipe in mouth and a big smile lighting up his famous face.

"Congratulations Teddy. What an achievement. You should be very proud of yourself."

I was speechless. I think I said thanks.

•••••

There were no mobile phones when I was growing up and creating havoc around St Joseph's View and other parts of Glanmire, on the outskirts of Cork city. A lot of homes didn't even have landlines. But news spread, somehow. The 'bush telegraph' they call it in Australia.

I could be out playing with a bunch of kids, boys and girls, somewhere on a green patch. Or I might be at home, banging a ball up against a wall. A shout would erupt from someone, somewhere.

"The Taoiseach is here." Jack Lynch might not even have been Taoiseach at the time but he was always the Taoiseach to us.

Michael McCarthy, who lived at the bottom of the terrace, was one of our older neighbours. He was a hurley maker who made hurleys for the likes of Christy Ring and Jack Lynch. McCarthy and Lynch were firm friends and, though Lynch had left Cork many decades before, the two men had remained close.

Lynch was friendly with many other men in the area. Whenever he visited Cork from his adopted home in Dublin, he would drive out to Glanmire and visit McCarthy. In the summer months they would sit outside McCarthy's on the stump of an old ash tree to chat. They would be joined by men like Bertie Murphy and the conversation would, inevitably, be about hurling.

They probably talked politics, too, but that didn't interest us.

As soon as I would hear that the Taoiseach was in McCarthy's I would gather up my hurley and ball, and chase off down the street, belting the ball in front of me. When I got to the end of the terrace I would make sure to hit the ball across the road towards the tree stump. I would go after it and hope that the men would notice, and that the great man might say something to me.

Of course, they knew what I was at. I did it every time he came, over a period of about ten years, so I wasn't very subtle.

One day, when I was about fourteen, Lynch came to visit. I went through my usual routine. This time, however, when I went to retrieve the ball Michael stopped me from chasing away.

"Hold it there young Mac, I want this man to see you properly," he said. Then he turned to the Taoiseach and continued, "Jack, this lad is going to be a good one."

"I'll look out for you, so," Jack Lynch said to me.

I ran off happier than I had ever been in my life.

•••••

As players and the team management, along with a growing number of county GAA officials, began to trickle back to the cramped dressing room, and the corridors around it, the celebrations began in earnest. The noise level was deafening. Jack Lynch's pride and delight in the success was a sight to behold.

Here was a man who had won six All-Ireland medals himself, five in hurling and one in football, and who had been at the centre of some of the major events in Irish history; this was the man who had guided the country through the potential catastrophe that was the Arms Crisis of the 1970s for Christ's sake; and he was shedding tears of joy at our achievement.

Bob Honohan squeezed past the mass of people. We hadn't seen each other on the field. Bob, a member of the selection committee, had been a mentor for me since the early 1980s. He had been a guiding hand. We had won three All-Ireland Under-21 titles together, with Bob as coach. We embraced briefly. Bob was bursting with pride. "The double, Teddy. I would never have dreamt it."

A month or so earlier, I feared that my dream had been shattered. I had watched the All-Ireland football semi-final from the living room of Oonagh's family home in Passage. Cork struggled to beat Roscommon. Mick McCarthy had come on as a sub and scored three points to waken the team up. They eventually won by seven points.

"What's up?" Oonagh's mother Phil asked me after the game. Everyone else was in great form, delighted with the win. All the talk was of 'the double'. I was showing no emotion at all.

"Come on, Teddy, out with it," she insisted.

"It's all this talk about the double," I admitted. "I don't think it's something I'm going to have to worry about."

I had missed the game because of a recurrence of ligament problems in my ankle. The problem had first surfaced in the middle of June. I had already lined out with the hurlers in two Championship games, beating Kerry and Waterford. I had also played with the footballers when we hammered Limerick in the Munster semi-final.

Billy had organised a weekend away for the footballers on the second weekend of June. We had games against Mayo on the Saturday, and Meath the following day. Billy and Fr Michael O'Brien, the new hurling manager, had worked out an agreement between them about how myself and Denis Walsh would train and we were allowed to travel with the footballers.

It was a welcome break from routine. I enjoyed the craic with the footballers. We had a fairly new hurling team for the 1990 Championship and I was still getting to know a lot of the players. I had known all of the footballers for the best part of ten years and we were a happy group.

These challenge games could be messy affairs but the selectors used them to monitor form and try out a few different variations. I was never a big fan of such games but, once they started, I always wanted to win. The competitive edge was always there and I would never hold back.

You couldn't hold back. There was so much competition for places on that team. Billy had four selectors – Bob, Christy Collins, Sean Murphy and Dave Loughman, who had coached me with the divisional team, Imokilly. We had won the county Championship together, in 1986.

They had chosen a strong team for the game against Mayo, who were preparing for the Connacht final. I was happy to be starting and I was determined to make an impression. I spotted a chance to use my ability in the air and went high for a ball. I caught it cleanly and came down. My right ankle crumbled beneath me. The ligaments were badly torn.

On the following Monday, back in Cork, the ankle was put in a cast and I was told to prepare for a five-week break. I couldn't believe it. What was I going to do with myself for five weeks if I wasn't playing football or hurling? I'd go mad. And probably drive everyone around me mad as well.

I was also thinking that I might find it hard to get my place back on either the football or hurling teams.

It wasn't that I lacked confidence. I was always confident playing either game. But I was realistic, too. There were brilliant players on the football panel that couldn't win regular places because of the competition. John O'Driscoll, one of the best footballers I ever played with, had been plagued by hamstring problems. I didn't even know what a hamstring was until I met John. His recurring problems meant he had to be happy a lot of the time with a substitute's role.

Mick McCarthy from Skibbereen was another brilliant footballer. He would have made any team in the country. In another time, he would have been the main man with Cork. But such was the number of good forwards available to Cork at the time Mick was not guaranteed a place on the team.

As well as that, Fr O'Brien was creating a new hurling team. For now, I was clearly a big part in his plans. But if the team started to win without me then there was always the possibility that he would opt against change. There was no thought of 'the double' at that time, I can assure you.

I missed both of the Munster finals. The footballers beat Kerry by fifteen points. The hurlers beat the reigning Munster and All-Ireland champions, Tipperary. Mark Foley, one of the newer guys, had been brilliant.

Foley was a big, rangy lad. I didn't know him too well, but he was a good lad. He had played in 1989 but probably hadn't the confidence to make a big impression then. It was obvious he had talent. Fr O'Brien knew him well. He had coached him at college level with Farranferris and was convinced Foley would play a big part for us in 1990.

I had known Fr O'Brien before he was appointed hurling manager, in late 1989. He had trained Sarsfields in 1982 and '83 and was a likeable man, but firm when he needed to be. The more I watched him over the years, the more I realised how shrewd he was.

Before I got injured I had played in a pre-Championship practise game in Pairc Ui Chaoimh involving all the panel members, with a few lads brought in to make up the numbers. Mark was centre-forward on one team. He was marked by my good friend, Jim Cashman, arguably the best hurler we had at the time. Now, I would have bet my life's savings at the time, if I'd had any, on Jim getting the better of any player in Ireland. Foley cleaned him out. And Jim never laid a hand on him.

I couldn't believe it. I asked Jim what he was at. "The Padre told me to take it easy. Mark has his final dentistry exams next week … and I had to make sure not to do any damage to his hands."

Jim wasn't convinced. Neither was I. Mark Foley was a good hurler and could take care of himself. He didn't need Jim to hold back.

The truth showed how clever Fr O'Brien was. Some of the other selectors had been arguing the case of a different player. I never found out who. It was a battle Fr O'Brien feared he was losing so he devised his plan. When Mark cleaned Jim out, Fr O'Brien didn't have to argue any more.

Mark scored 2-7 against Tipperary in the Munster final. The Padre had been vindicated.

Brendan O'Sullivan, one of the nicest guys in hurling, had been on the fringes of the team for a while without making the breakthrough. Now, I was sitting at home nursing my ankle and Brendan was playing out of his skin. I was delighted for him in one way. But what effect would it have when I started playing again?

The entire county of Cork was on a high. And here was Teddy, with his foot stuck in plaster, going out of his mind with boredom and worry. I had played a small part as a substitute in the hurling semi-final victory over Antrim but the ankle wasn't right and I was back on the treatment table. I hounded Dr Con Murphy, our popular medic. I drove the physios mad. I went back training against advice. I was being the Teddy they all knew, listening to nobody, stubborn as a mule.

Fr O'Brien and his coach, Gerald McCarthy, had been a little sympathetic to my plight and included me on the panel for the game with Antrim. Billy was encouraging but also warned me against doing too much. After watching the football semi-final despondently from Passage, on the afternoon of August 12, I checked the fixtures calendar. The hurling final would be played on September 2. That gave me three weeks. Those could be the most important weeks of my life.

Those weeks were typical of the way my life had evolved. Everything else, and I mean everything, was secondary to my effort to proving myself fit enough to play in the All-Ireland hurling final.

Oonagh was pregnant with Cian, but my health and well-being came first. Okay, no one was being silly and Oonagh was getting the best of care. But when the day-to-day condition of either one of us was occupying anyone's attention it was Teddy's ankle, and not Oonagh's unborn baby, that was the first subject for a question.

This was a man playing in an All-Ireland final. That happens only once a year. Maybe twice, but only in exceptional circumstances. As it happened, those were my circumstances. Babies are born every day, the lads would joke. In the last few weeks of August it was a joke you could get away with. Just.

Work at the Beamish & Crawford plant was hectic. This was holiday time and the demand for the products was at its highest. It was an important time for the company which employed a lot of people in Cork. My colleagues shouldered more than their burden so that I could devote as much time as possible to making a full recovery. It was a reminder, if one was needed, that I was representing more than my family and my club. I was representing everyone at Beamish & Crawford, as well.

There were duties that I could have tended to at home, with my mother in Glanmire, but she resolutely put everything on hold. My brothers and sisters would silently acknowledge a reality that had been evident for ten years, or more – Mam's clock kept time with Teddy's training and playing. It was never more evident than in the August of 1990.

Every morning I felt better. I hated the physiotherapy when it hurt, but I knew it was working so I'd put up with it. I wasn't the best time-keeper normally, but when the physios had time for me I was there. Dr Con was amazed. Teddy was Mr Reliable. Dr Con and the entire medical team were also a great source of support and encouragement. I couldn't have made it without them.

Who would have believed it? Here was the kid who had almost blown his career before it started. If you had talked history to me then – it was only four years earlier – I would probably have shot back with some comment about living for the now. Yet, here I was, dedicating myself to a regime that would allow me to return to action a lot quicker than should have been possible.

To this day, I'm not sure what happened between Billy and Fr O'Brien.

Naturally, both were thinking of their own team first, but there was never a clash or a contest that I was aware of.

The week after the football semi-final was an anxious one for me. In the grand scheme of things it was a quiet week but, on a personal level, it was probably the worst. I just wasn't sure how I could possibly figure in the hurling final, and the football final was still too far away to be sure of anything. What kept me going was the attitude of the management teams and the players. No questions were raised. I was part of both squads and treated the same as everyone else. That meant I would be given the same chance as everyone else. It was the motivation I needed.

Week two was different.

It was media week for the hurling final. Photographers and TV crews descended on Cork. We were well used to the presence of the local media – as the second city in Ireland we had the *Examiner* and the *Evening Echo* as well as a number of regional newspapers, like *The Southern Star* and the *Imokilly People*. We knew the lads involved with them. The All-Ireland final drew a much larger media presence. Cork's bid for a double increased that presence, and my bid for a special place in the history of the GAA added a further element of interest.

I think it is a tribute to a lot of people, like Fr O'Brien, Billy and Frank Murphy, that I was well protected, though not completely unaware, of the mania that was building up. Some of the journalists were helpful. There were decent guys like Mick Dunne from RTÉ, and Paddy Downey and Peadar O'Brien involved with the national media, based in Dublin. Jim O'Sullivan had the highest profile of the Cork-based journalists, along with Michael Ellard. There were a couple of younger guys from the Dublin papers, nearer enough to my age, whom I got along with. I was newsworthy and they needed me. But they respected me, as well. The attention was pressurised but it didn't become oppressive.

There was another factor that I only understood later which added to the attention and the focus on my adventure. Ireland had been gripped with a sort of fever during that summer, when the Republic of Ireland played in the World Cup finals in Italy. This was the period when their manager Jack Charlton was the most high-profile figure in Irish life. Sport became headline news on television, radio and in the newspapers.

We were all caught up in it. Training times were shifted so that we could watch the games involving Ireland. In some cases, the times of games should have been changed because everyone was so clued in to the soccer. The effect on us would only be felt when the World Cup ended.

People had been so caught up in the drama of Italia '90 that they sought another diversion as soon as it was over. They found their replacement drug in the GAA Championships. Men and women who had never before had an interest in the national games began to notice. They wanted information and soaked up as much as possible.

Because our situation in Cork was so unique, and my own situation in particular was so significant, we became the focus of attention. Many people in the GAA had feared that Ireland's success in International soccer would damage Gaelic games. The fact was that the national games thrived as a result of the greater interest generated in sport in general.

More important than all of that, at the time, was that my ankle had responded to the urgings of the physiotherapists. I began to feel really good ten days before the hurling final. I was running completely without pain and I was landing from my leaps without any twinge. I wasn't even thinking about the ankle. That was the crunch: I was training now without inhibition. Fr O'Brien and Gerald McCarthy told me they had noticed it. Billy Morgan kept in touch without ever putting on any pressure. "Keep it going," was his advice.

No one told me that I would be named on the team to start the final but you do get a sense in training about what way the management team is thinking. I was only twenty-five years old but I was already one of the senior members of the squad. Fr O'Brien and Gerald expected me to take responsibility and I was doing that in training. Without being cocky or complacent, I just felt comfortable that I had trained myself back into the starting fifteen.

Since we had last won an All-Ireland hurling title in 1986, we had lost some great players. Legends of the game, like Jimmy Barry Murphy, had retired. Others who had gone were Tom Cashman, Johnny Crowley, John Fenton, Pat Hartnett and Denis Mulcahy. Our goalkeeper, Ger Cunningham, Denis Walsh, Jim Cashman, Tony O'Sullivan, Tomas Mulcahy, Kevin Hennessy,

Ger Fitzgerald, John Fitzgibbon and myself were the only guys still around.

My clubmate, John Considine, had come into the team that year and quickly established himself as a first-choice back. Sean O'Gorman was a very experienced player who had actually played full-forward the year before, but became a vital part of our defence in 1990. Sean McCarthy, Kieran McGuckin, Brendan O'Sullivan, Mark Foley, Cathal Casey and David Quirke all began to establish themselves. There wasn't room for everyone on the starting fifteen, but each player had a defined role.

It has to be remembered that, at the start of 1990, Cork hurling was in a difficult place. We had been eclipsed in Munster by Tipperary. In the 1989 Championship we had been well beaten by Waterford in a first-round replay and we had started the summer of 1990 as outsiders for any titles. Earlier in the year, we had been hammered by Wexford in a League game in Nowlan Park and I remember players shedding tears of frustration.

We were still outsiders in the build-up to the All-Ireland final. Galway had a vastly experienced team who had won the Championship in 1987 and '88, and were men with a mission in 1990. They had been engulfed in controversy the previous year when their centre half-back, Tony Keady, was suspended for twelve months for playing without proper authorisation in the New York Championship. It had become a major distraction. They felt victimised and were determined to get justice by winning the Championship, in 1990.

They must wonder today how they made such a mess of it, though we can take some of the credit.

I have always valued Jim Cashman's friendship. I have also admired him as one of the greatest hurlers I have ever played with. For the first 35 minutes of the 1990 All-Ireland final I, along with hurling followers everywhere, felt sympathy for Jim. He was marking Joe Cooney and he was getting fleeced.

That first half was quite incredible. We played well. Cooney just played better. We got the perfect start with a goal from Kevin Hennessy. I got an early point. The action was unrelenting. Brendan and myself had a great battle with Pat Malone and Michael Coleman in midfield. There was no time to think about anything; we played on instinct and I think that made it a good game.

We had a little fortune on our side. Galway missed a couple of good goal chances. They actually scored one but the referee, John Moore, had already blown his whistle to award a free. To Galway. Cooney got a point from the free but a goal would have been a real boost to them.

We were five points down at half time, 1-8 to 1-13, and we felt lucky. Fr O'Brien and Gerald McCarthy showed their mettle at half time. There was no panic. They weren't shouting and roaring, they were calm and reassuring. Jim, I'm sure though he has never said it, expected to be replaced. He wasn't. The management kept faith in him. They made a few positional changes, bringing Tomas 'Mul' out to the half-forward line. Ger would add some length to his puck outs to try and take their half-back line out of the game. Small things; simple things. All very effective.

Jim had a much better second half. Cooney was subdued. Mul scored an early goal. Ger made an incredibly brave save with his face! If Galway had got a goal then we would probably have been beaten.

We scored four goals in that second half. I scored my third point of the game and we won by just three points, 5-15 to 2-21. You don't often see that sort of scoreline in an All-Ireland final.

Talk of the double began immediately. I didn't partake. As I've already indicated, I took it easy with the celebrations. Even if I was tempted to overdo things, I would remember that Billy would be waiting for me on the Thursday night in training and I would suffer for any excesses.

In fairness to Morgan, he never interfered. He understood the need for me to enjoy the hurling success. A few beers were not going to affect the sort of fitness I had built up in six seasons of involvement at inter-county level.

•••••

I did make one error that would serve as a lesson to me.

It was traditional for All-Ireland final teams to attend a reception at Beamish & Crawford on the Tuesday following the game. This would always be a special event for me since I was an employee of the company. It was said in Cork that if they'd sold tickets for the reception they could have got £1,000 each.

I was lucky that my career in the company was going well. After a few years of driving a forklift and working on the production line I had been given an opportunity to work with the sales team at Beamish. That added even more significance to the reception in 1990. I didn't appreciate that. While the other players arrived kitted out in the official blazer and slacks, along with collar and tie, I turned up in a pair of Parazone bleached jeans and a jumper. My hair was all over the place and the razor I had used that morning must have been a little blunt. I knew immediately that I had made a mistake. I should have been aware that I was more than a Cork hurler that day. I was also part of the Beamish & Crawford sales team, the public face of one of the biggest companies in Cork. There was nothing I could do at that stage. I just had to get on with it.

I was back at work on Thursday. The Area Manager I worked with was Michael Barrett and we were at a meeting in his office when the phone rang, at about 9.30am. It was the Sales Director, John Beasley. He wanted to see me. Michael didn't know why. "Maybe he wants to welcome you to the sales team," he speculated. I wasn't so sure. John was a nice man but I suspected he wasn't happy with me. He was standing with his back to the open door looking out the window when I knocked. Without saying hello he began talking. "Teddy, Tuesday was a great day, wasn't it?"

Before I got a chance to nod in agreement he said something like, "It's a pity you were a disgrace to Beamish & Crawford. You think there is only one team in Cork and you're right. That team is Beamish & Crawford. It might be time to review your position in Sales."

A cold sweat came over me. I was freezing with fright. What had I done? Was I sacked? I left his office in a daze. Michael Barrett met me and asked me how I'd got on. "I didn't," was all I could mumble. I ran out of the place, jumped into my white Datsun Bluebird and drove away. I had calls to make but I was in no fit state to work. Later I phoned Michael and asked him what the situation was. He told me John was annoyed but that everything would be okay.

It was the second big fright of my life. The first had been the threat of expulsion from North Mon after failing to turn up for a game.

Beamish & Crawford was a brilliant company to work for. I got on with everyone, from the tele-sales girls to the Managing Director. The lads I worked with were brilliant. In the years I was doing shift work on the floor the lads would help. If I was on the evening shift, from 4pm to midnight, they knew I would be training at 7pm and they would cover for me. If I was on nights, midnight to 8am, they would tell me to go home around 3am when most of the heavy work was done so that I could get a proper night's sleep if there was a match coming up on the Sunday. They took up the slack.

Management couldn't officially approve that sort of thing but I'm sure they knew it was happening and they turned a blind eye to it. They were as proud of my successes as the lads I worked with were. And that was why John Beasley was so annoyed with me. He was right. I hadn't shown proper respect to my work mates and my employers. It never happened again.

•••••

I trained with the footballers on that Thursday night. At the first sign of sweat on my forehead the slagging started. "I can smell the booze coming out of you," Niall Cahalane roared laughing.

"He'll do the double alright … double whiskeys."

The banter had begun as soon as I arrived at the ground that evening. Because of my injury and my involvement with the hurlers, I hadn't been around the footballers much that summer. The first man I met was John 'Kid' Cronin, officially our kit man but a person who gave a ferocious commitment to Cork football and hurling. He was a great friend of all the players and I valued his friendship and good humour. As we exchanged greetings I asked him if there were any new faces around the place.

"There's only the one," he answered.

"Who's that?" I asked in all innocence.

"You." he said and went off laughing.

There wasn't much danger of losing the run of yourself with this lot around.

I was thinking about the double. It preyed on my mind. I tried to set it aside but it was impossible to avoid. In a way, I wasn't comfortable with it because I wondered if I deserved it ahead of all those great players who had played both hurling and football for Cork. I didn't confide in anyone. Maybe

I should have. I worked through it myself.

My focus had to be on the football final only. That wasn't easy because, every waking minute of the day, there was some reminder about the historic potential of my participation in the football final. By the time we gathered in Cork on the Saturday morning before the game for the train journey to Dublin, however, my head was straight. The lads helped. The jokes about the double had stopped soon after they began. They knew I wanted to think about the game only. I was just another player, happy to be part of the team.

I looked at some of the guys around me who would not be starting. Paddy Hayes, who had soldiered with me at Under-21 level and missed a lot of time with injury, was back in the panel. John O'Driscoll, who I have already described as one of the best footballers I played with. And John Cleary, another brilliant forward. All in the subs. Great players. Really great. I knew I was lucky.

It was strange, in a way. I had not played with Cork in the Championship since May 27, when we beat Limerick. Now, here I was ready to wear the No.12 jersey in the All-Ireland final.

We had played Meath in three previous All-Ireland finals, including a replay, in 1987 and '88. I had never found them particularly tough or hard affairs but they had gained almost legendary status in Irish sport for levels of rancour that I could never measure.

Colm O'Neill was the unlucky guy in 1990. From the hurling stronghold of Midleton, Colm was a super footballer and proved that with a brilliant scoring performance in the Munster final. He kicked eleven points that day, eight of them from frees. He was desperately unlucky not to score a goal in the All-Ireland final and watched a great shot come back off the crossbar. If that had gone in I think it would have been a different game. We would have won it handily.

Instead, Colm and Mick Lyons got involved just before half time. Colm retaliated. Paddy Russell, the referee, sent him off. It was a personal disappointment for Colm but it acted as a spur to the team, just as it always does when a team is reduced to fourteen men. We all redoubled our efforts.

Shea Fahy gave his greatest performance since transferring from Kildare. Our other import from Kildare, Larry Tompkins, produced levels of courage that are hard to comprehend at this remove. He shouldn't have been able to stand up, never mind play in an All-Ireland final, after suffering a cruciate ligament injury to his knee early in the game. He kicked four points and was a constant inspiration. We didn't even know he was hurt until the game was over.

We also needed some heroics from our goalkeeper, just like in the hurling final. This time it was John Kerins who produced a brave save at a crucial stage in the second half which prevented Brian Stafford from scoring what could have been a match-changing goal.

We won by 0-11 to 0-9. The Sam Maguire Cup was presented to Larry and I sat in the dark old dressing room in the corner of the old Hogan Stand with my hero, Jack Lynch.

•••••

There is something special about the homecoming to Cork after an All-Ireland win. I experienced it four times and it was better each time. After my first senior win in 1986, I craved the experience again. I was lucky to experience it three more times. You know something – it is possibly better than winning the match itself.

We were usually based at The Burlington Hotel in Dublin in those days, though, in 1990, we were shifted to the Royal Marine Hotel in Dun Laoghaire. It wasn't convenient to our usual haunts but in the euphoria that followed achieving the double nothing really mattered except the celebration.

As that Sunday night grew into the early hours of the Monday morning I began to think about the journey home. I wished the hours away so that we could get to Heuston Station and board the train. Those were the days when the two teams were brought together for lunch the following day. I generally enjoyed meeting opponents on those occasions, but, in 1990, I do remember looking at my watch more often than usual. I wanted to get back to Cork.

I was also getting more attention than I wanted. I was nearly hoarse from talking, answering the same questions with the same answers, over and over again. I didn't want to talk about me. I wanted a few pints and a laugh. I knew when I got on the train I would be with the lads, and we'd have a few crates of beer and plenty of craic.

I could picture how the journey would unfold. The reality was even better. Heuston Station was a riot of colour. Red and white flags – the emblems of Canada and Japan, as well as the Confederate flag amongst them – were carried by ecstatic supporters who cheered us onto the platform and the train.

In Charleville Station, our supporters had gathered and gave us a rousing reception. We stopped in Mallow and the people had gathered in their thousands. In Kent Station in Cork, we were met with an explosion of noise. I reflected on the homecoming of two weeks previously. It had been memorable. This was at another level altogether.

We eventually got to the open-topped bus. As we left the station we couldn't believe our eyes. Every sense was alert. You could smell the atmosphere rather than feel it. There were people everywhere. It was mind-boggling. They hung off lampposts and chimneys.

We drove up McCurtain Street, against the regular traffic flow, and around Paddy Barry's corner off Bridge Street and then faced into Patrick Street where an estimated 40,000 people awaited us. It was breathtaking. Young lads ran in front of the bus as it snaked its way up to a platform. You would be terrified they would fall under the bus. Everyone of them survived.

I spotted some famous faces. Ray Cummins stood with his family clapping happily. One of the greatest ever dual players was saluting us as a common man. My spirits soared ever higher with the honour.

Then, near the stage that had been erected to host us, I saw Jimmy Barry Murphy. He looked at me and gave a thumbs up. I returned it. My heart was bursting.

On the platform we were introduced, one by one. Each player received a tremendous cheer. When my turn came they went wild. I was absolutely humbled. I was a little glad that it was dark because tears were filling my eyes.

It was a relief when the attention shifted to Larry with the Sam Maguire Cup. Then Tomas Mul was called to bring the Liam MacCarthy Cup onto the stage. Cork went absolutely crazy. It was a moment no one who was there will ever forget.

I stood back to take it all in.

It was some journey getting here, Teddy boy, I thought to myself.

CHAPTER**2**

FAMILY MATTERS

My earliest memories are amongst those I cherish most because they are the only memories I have of my father. He died on March 11, 1970, when I was just four years old.

Not that I remember much. He was ailing at home for what seemed a long time, as cancer sucked the life out of him. It was a devastating blow to my mother Mary who was left with eight children to look after. We ranged in age from one to sixteen.

In fairness, the older ones tended to look after themselves and helped out with looking after the youngest in the family which included myself, my older brother Denis and the youngest of us all, my sister, Mary.

Denis McCarthy, my father, was from a family originally from Bandon in West Cork. He had a future planned out for him by his self-educated father. An uncle was a successful doctor in London and intended bringing my father and his brothers and sister to England to be educated. But he died in his 30s and that plan fell through.

My father's family moved to Glanmire. It was there that he met Mary O'Keeffe and she was his match for life, a life cut tragically short by his illness. Coincidentally, all of my mother's family had gone to England but she returned home after six months and settled into life as a housewife.

Dad worked for a time with the Gas Company and eventually was employed during the construction of St Stephen's Hospital on the Sarsfield Road, in Glanmire. When the hospital construction was completed he got a job there in maintenance, employed by what was then the Southern Health Board. It was the place where he died and it was also where my mother would find employment when she became the family bread-winner after his death.

It was a seriously tough time, especially for my mother. Two weeks after my father's death my grandfather, who lived just down the road, died. We had nothing. There were mornings when we quite simply did not have anything to eat for breakfast. We knew nothing of the finer things in life.

What we did have was a great community around us. Those were the days when doors, front and back, were always open. If you were short of milk or butter or bread, you just went next door. We could pop into O'Dwyers, McCarthy's, Corcoran's or Walsh's any time we wanted anything.

If you didn't have the money for other needs the local shops would provide credit. They didn't hound my mother for payment either, though she always paid her debts. That wasn't pride; it was a sense of duty. You treated people as you would wish to be treated yourself.

When my father was ill the local people raised sufficient money to send him on a pilgrimage to Lourdes. That was the way people lived then. People didn't pity us, they just looked after us. When my mother and older brothers and sisters were out working, the neighbours would look after Denis, Mary and me. They didn't have to be asked. It was the natural way of things.

As Denis and I got a bit older I suspect we were almost impossible to look out for. We didn't want looking after, but the neighbours tried anyway.

We lived in St Joseph's View in Glanmire. I was born on July 1, 1965, the seventh in the family and christened Thaddeus. It was a traditional name on my father's side of the family. My Uncle Ted was also christened Thaddeus. My name was shortened early in life and I was called Teddy to differentiate me from Ted.

My older brothers, Pat and Michael, were already budding sportsmen; Denis was just two years older. My sisters Breda, Ellen and Philly were delighted to have a newborn to look after. Mary was born four years later.

Our lives were changed completely by the death of our father. The older children went to work after completing National School. My mother would have preferred if they could have continued their education but that choice just wasn't available. I was the first in the family to go on to secondary school and complete my Leaving Certificate. It was one of the early signs that whatever good fortune would fall on the McCarthy family in those years would come in my direction.

It would be unfair to my mother's memory and to the efforts of the older children and our neighbours to describe a life of destitution. Yes, we were hungry at times and it was a struggle but we always survived. We were poor and there is no shame in that. Going to school we often had to be satisfied with a few biscuits to be shared between break and lunch.

My memories of some of the earliest days in school are hazy but Denis clearly recalls Ellen being given charge of a box of biscuits at the start of each week. Mam just didn't have the money to make sandwiches for us all. We all took it in turns to choose which were our favourites. The chocolate biscuit was the most sought after. We ate two for break, two for lunch. We might have wanted more to eat but we knew we couldn't have it. That was our life and we put up with it.

What I found the most difficult was the loneliness. No one was to blame for that. It was circumstances. I had great brothers and sisters, great friends, but they were often preoccupied with other important things in life and I felt as a kid that I was missing out on something not having a father.

It is hard to be specific about what exactly I was missing. But I do remember weekends when I would be lying out in the garden looking up at the sky and not having anyone to play with. It was just because the neighbours and my friends were gone to the beach for the day or on some other outing. We didn't have those outings because we could not afford it or my mother would be working.

There were Saturdays when I would spend hours just belting a ball up against a gable wall, playing mini-games with myself. I often wished we could go on summer holidays like everyone else but it wasn't to be. If I was feeling sorry for myself I knew better than to complain. My mother and the others were fighting the battle for survival and there was no time to make my worries their worries.

In some ways I was lucky. It is beautiful in Glanmire, and it was even more beautiful then. We could live the outdoor life. The river was a source of adventure and we had the GAA grounds, home of Sarsfields Hurling Club and Glanmire Football Club. Two different names, two separate clubs, but the one entity. Facilities were shared. If you played with Sarsfields then you automatically played football with Glanmire. We didn't have a clubhouse then. There was a shed where all the equipment was stored. We used the natural amenities of the area. The Butlerstown River flowed beside the pitch and that was our shower and our bath.

During the summer months, and on Saturdays during school term, we spent most of our time on the pitch creating our own entertainment. We would play cricket and soccer. We didn't play a lot of hurling and football during the day because we would be back down on the pitch in the evening training with the clubs.

That pitch was a sanctuary for Denis and myself. It was also a place of torture for Breda and Ellen because of our antics. Many Saturday nights during the summer the two older girls would be put in charge of ensuring that we went to bed early if my mother was working the 4pm to midnight shift at the hospital. The procedure was that we would have our bath around 5.30pm – one bath would do the lot of us – and then Denis and I would go to bed at 6pm, or 7pm at the latest.

This gave the girls time to have their own bath and to get ready to go out for the night, socialising.

The problem for the girls was that the local pitch was the venue for many Cork junior championship games at the time. You could hear the roar of the crowd from the house which was just one hundred yards away as the crow flies. As soon as we knew that either Breda or Ellen was in the bath we would slip into our mother's bedroom at the front of the house, climb out the top window, down onto the porch, jump to the ground and race down to the pitch.

When they went to check up on us and found the beds empty they knew where we were. But when they came down to the pitch after us we would hide in the crowd and they could never get us. That delayed many a planned night out.

It was on those nights, too, that I first got a taste of the atmosphere surrounding a game of football or hurling. I could feel the buzz of excitement and anticipation of the people at the game. The men were frightening. There was a toughness, a hardness about them. The crowd would be baying. The roars that greeted big challenges or scores were exciting for me.

Any thoughts our sisters might have had of retribution the following morning for our antics were obliterated by my mother's presence. In her bosom I was safe. I didn't know it then, but she was already displaying in her own special way her affection and her protectiveness of me which would become more and more obvious as I grew up.

In the absence of a father I was lucky that there were others willing to provide a protective hand in those vital early years of growing up. I probably didn't always show my appreciation and it was only when I was older that I realised just how important these people would be in my life.

•••••

Every boy should remember his first pair of boots. I certainly do. They were Gola boots, hardly the sexiest things around. They were black with a luminous, high-visibility green stripe on them. They were my most loved possession. To this day I remember them fondly.

I was eight years old when I got them. We had a match on a Saturday and, on the night before, the front door opened and a familiar voice shouted "Hello ... anyone at home?" Mam and I were in the kitchen when Mickey Barry came in. He had a parcel in his hand. "For you, Teddy," he said, "you can wear them tomorrow."

I tore open the wrapping, almost shivering with excitement. It was a scene familiar to my mother. Mickey had done this before for our family. It was one of the many decent and unforgettable things that he did for us in our childhood. It wasn't just the McCarthy's that Mickey looked after. Anyone in Glanmire who was in need could depend on him and his family.

Mickey was a brother of Pat Barry, the great Sarsfields and Cork player of the 1950s who captained the county to All-Ireland success in 1952. We all knew him as Pat though, countrywide, he was known as Paddy having been given that name by the great GAA commentator Micheal O'Hehir. In whatever success Sarsfields enjoyed in the second half of the 20th century, the Barry's were heavily involved.

Mickey was Mr Sarsfields. The GAA is a lucky organisation that it has men like him in small parishes all over the country utterly dedicated to providing sporting opportunities for young boys and girls. Their only reward is watching those young boys and girls get some enjoyment from the games and, maybe, from time to time, climb the ranks and reach the top. Paddy Duggan was another man who dedicated himself, selflessly, to coaching us youngsters.

Mickey did all the administration for the senior club and still had time to train the juvenile teams. Wednesday was his half-day from the family bakery he ran with his brother. He would mow the pitch and line it. When that was done we would be arriving home from school and he would conduct a training session.

He was the man who organised our games against neighbouring clubs. He also provided transport in the bakery's van. We fought like lunatics to get into the van because Mickey would always ensure that there would be a supply of buns and cakes in the corner. It might not have been the best preparation for a game, but at least he knew we would not be a noisy bunch on the journey, we were too busy munching.

He was our trainer, our manager, our mentor and our disciplinarian. Mickey knew everything that went on amongst the kids around Glanmire. He knew when there were rows and who caused them. He knew the personalities of all the children and he seemed to have an uncanny knack of dealing with each and every one of them.

He recognised that from an early age I could be stubborn when I didn't get my own way, especially if a sporting contest or an incident in that contest did not result in my favour. I had a temper, too, and easily became involved in fights. He taught me some early lessons about my behaviour.

One day, in a practise game, I decided to go on strike, a mini-protest for some cause that is now long forgotten. I was being my most stubborn and bloody awkward and I lay down on the pitch and wouldn't move, expecting the game to be stopped so that negotiations could begin.

I thought, at the very least, that Mickey might come over and give me a clatter or perhaps take me on in an argument, and then I could let him have a piece of my mind. He did nothing. The game went on. The play went on around me as if I wasn't there and that was worse than anything. Eventually, I just got up and sheepishly rejoined the game. He had beaten me psychologically, proving to me that the world would not stop just because I didn't get my way.

It is not a lesson I learned easily. I was headstrong and aggressive on the field, and off it. There were regular fights over petty things. We'd often play a game on The Green after school where there was a rule that if you were not there at the start you wouldn't be picked. I would race home from school, ignoring the slice of bread and jam my mother would have ready for me, to make sure I was there on time. If I didn't make it and wasn't picked I would wait for the ball to come near me and I would kick it over the ditch.

On the days when I was playing I would create trouble, too. There was one incident that I am reminded of to this day. Boys and girls played together and Lily Zinkant was a regular participant in our games. She was a couple of years older than me and had just as much ability as I had. That would lead to friction if she happened to get the better of me. I didn't like being second best. We would end up fighting like two boys.

One day, the fight went too far. Maybe I went too far and Lily was hurt. Her father was furious when he found out and called to the house to complain. It was a journey familiar to a number of parents in the area. I remember hearing that Mr Zinkant was on the warpath and I hid under the kitchen table. He was furious, but Mam intervened. She knew I was probably in the wrong, but she believed in the sanctity of the home and would not allow someone to come in and punish me.

When he left, however, she left me in no doubt that I was not to do the same thing again. It was another lesson that I took a bit of time to learn.

The older children in the family had all attended Riverstown National School. After my father died and my mother went back to work she had to make a decision. She would not be able to accompany us to and from school every day, and Riverstown was on the busy main Cork to Dublin road. So Breda, Ellen, Philly, Denis, Mary and I were sent to Brook Lodge National

School. It was another stroke of luck.

Mr O'Connor was our first principal in Brook Lodge and he was a kindly man who looked after us. He retired when I was going into fourth class and a new principal was appointed. He was Tim Glavin from Ballyhooley, near Fermoy. He was wonderful for us in every way. He understood the difficulties we had at home but never patronised us. He was kind and thoughtful. We couldn't afford Encyclopedia Brittanica but somehow he got us a full set.

He was also a good man to talk to. He still is. I wasn't that interested in school subjects. I wanted to be outdoors, playing hurling and football. He encouraged and cajoled me, providing the sort of guidance that I needed at the time.

Tim also organised a competition in hurling and football between four schools in the area. While we had always played amongst ourselves, there had never been games between schools up to that time. It was as good as an All-Ireland Championship to us. I loved it, especially because we won it each year for my remaining three years at the school.

My competitive streak was already a thing of renown around Glanmire. However, through playing with Brook Lodge, and with Sarsfields, I was beginning to attract the notice of hurling enthusiasts around the East Cork area, from as early as the age of eight.

Every spare moment was spent with a hurley and a ball, either at the house or down at the pitch. I would convince Denis to come to the pitch with me every evening and get him to stand behind one goal. I would spend half an hour or more taking frees from all sorts of angles. I suspect I was only standing on the 21 yard line, but it showed that I was determined to make the best of whatever natural talent I had.

Everywhere I walked I brought the hurley with me. It was like a walking stick. I would walk up the terrace, belting the ball against the wall, time and again.

There was hurling and football in the blood. My father and all of his brothers played at club level. My mother had an uncle who played for Limerick. My older brothers, Pat and Michael, were already playing senior with Sarsfields and Glanmire, and Denis was probably the most enthusiastic of all of us. His problem was that at the age of about 18, when he should have had time for training and playing, he was out working, helping out the family. Of the girls, only Ellen played camogie, but she was really talented and played under-age for Cork.

Some of the toughest games I played back then as a kid were in the garden on a Sunday. Pat and Michael would be there. I would be paired with Michael, Denis with Pat. There was nothing spared. You had to be tough. Nothing was broken except for a few windows.

Michael did come to the notice of the Cork minor selectors in 1971. He was called for trials and was a member of the extended squad. Another member of that squad was a lad named Jimmy Barry Murphy, who was embarking on what turned out to be a glorious sporting career. I don't remember Michael hurling but people around here recall a stylish player who could strike the ball long distances. The older men thought he had potential as a county man.

However, the search for employment was never ending and would curtail whatever chance Michael had of playing for Cork beyond the minor grade. At the age of 20, he married an English girl, Marie, and they moved to England. It wasn't something that had a major impact on us. He came home from time to time to play for the club and we never felt that he was that far away.

He was convinced to come home for one memorable hurling occasion. In 1975, the Sarsfields Under-21 team reached the Cork County Championship 'A' Final. Pat was a member of the team all that summer and when it came to the final everyone knew that Michael could make a difference. He was working in Manchester at the time and it wasn't easy to get time off.

He and Marie also had a son, John by then and that added to the complications. What would happen if he got injured? Who would bring in the family income then? Michael weighed up all considerations and risks and made the only decision possible. He came home for the weekend to play in the county final. Sarsfields won.

I don't remember the game and have only a faint recollection of the celebrations around Glanmire on the Sunday night. Michael went back to Manchester on the Monday. It was the last time I saw him.

Less than a year later Michael was taken from us. He was managing a pub in Manchester and, one night, after locking up he took a lift home in the back of a van. There was an accident. Michael was thrown through the back door of the van. He died soon after from his injuries.

I don't remember very much about it. Maybe it's because I was just ten years old and too young to comprehend. Maybe it's because I don't want to remember.

What I do recall is my mother's anguish. She had been so strong and so resolute after my father's death. It broke her heart but she never allowed it to break her will. She had shouldered the whole family through that terrible time. Michael's death was a blow too many.

Again the community came to our aid. Funds were raised to send the entire family to Manchester, except for Denis who was preparing for Confirmation. Neighbours and friends travelled to provide emotional and physical support. They tried to give comfort to my mother, but this time she could not be comforted.

Mam wanted Michael's body to be brought home for burial. But Marie had a young son and she was staying in Manchester and wanted her husband buried there. That caused some tension, though I wasn't aware of it at the time.

It does hurt me now that Marie and John are back living in Cork, and Michael is in a grave in Manchester, all alone. His death had a terrible affect on my mother. She struggled to cope with the loss of a child. It became a difficult time for us all, especially Mary and myself, who were living at home with her. Denis had already started working by then and was often working nights.

There were days when she had a tipple or two. We were too young to understand what was going on and that made life at home difficult at times. I don't blame her for that. She was dealt a bloody lousy hand in life. She was the perfect mother in so many other ways. I know that better than anyone.

It took her a long time to recover and, as soon as she had, life delivered another series of blows that were just bloody unfair and awful.

CHAPTER**3**

SCHOOL OF HARD KNOCKS

My sisters played a huge part in my early life. Ellen was six years older and a natural sportswoman. She was a super hurler and I think that created a natural affinity between us.

When Pat moved away, first to England and then to Shanbally to the south of the city, following Michael's death, Ellen took over as my mentor at home. She and Philly were working in Punch's factory in Glanmire and she would come home in the evening, have her dinner and then bring me out into the garden where she honed my skills. She didn't hold back in the physical stakes either. I would get away with nothing.

Ellen was very talented. She played locally with Sarsfields, and the Cork minor selectors rewarded her talent. More than anyone she inspired me to practise my skills and she instilled in me the desire to be a successful sportsman. Because some of my abilities came naturally I probably didn't appreciate them. She made sure I understood how lucky I was, and that I should do everything to develop those skills.

As well as helping me as a young footballer and hurler, Ellen was also playing her part in providing distractions for me. I was full of energy, always wanting to be on the go, looking for something to do. As already mentioned, I had a habit of getting into scrapes with other kids around Glanmire and my mother was constantly defending me.

One escape I was fortunate to have was at Breda's new home in Annacarton, a townland beside Glanmire. She had married Peter Holland who ran a 30-acre farm there. It seemed like 1,000 acres to me. It was heaven. I loved it and remember every moment spent there with great affection.

Brought up on a terrace in a suburb of a big city, I took to the land like a natural. From the age of ten to twelve I spent my summers out there with Breda, Peter and their two daughters, Michelle and Deirdre. Peter grew vegetables and kept some dry stock, and he had a willing helper when I was around.

We started work at daylight, feeding the cattle, bringing in the hay, ploughing fields. I learned to drive the tractor and I helped bring the cattle to the mart, and watched the art of buying and selling with fascination. This was a whole new world to me, yet I felt at home.

The best day of the week was Friday when Peter would load up the trailer with vegetables – cabbage, carrots and potatoes – and drive to the supermarket in Mayfield. It was called Mayfair and the manager there was a man named Declan Guckian.

Peter and Declan treated me like a man. They included me in their conversations, especially when the subject was hurling or football. Peter became a father-figure to me. He was also a very good friend to my mother.

I clearly remember the Saturday morning when I was twelve years old and Breda woke me at three o'clock in the morning. It was during the school term but I was spending the weekend with them. Peter had become ill during the night and had to go to hospital. He was diagnosed with a tumour on the brain.

Peter asked my school principal, Tim Glavin, if I could take two weeks off school to run the farm while he began chemotherapy. As expected, Tim agreed to the request and I took my responsibility seriously. I think now, looking back on it, that I began to grow up a little bit then.

I'm not so sure Mary thought that. When I returned home we fought constantly, and I mean 'fought'. Punches were thrown. I'm not proud of that and I'm not going to offer excuses. There was constant tension. I know she hated me. She told me so, not just then but later in life.

I fought with Denis, too, even when I knew I would come off worst. It always happened when Mam was on the late shift at the hospital. We broke chairs and windows and spent the minutes before she came home trying to patch up the place as best we could.

The one thing we never broke was the television. No matter how hot our tempers flared we made sure the TV was safe. We had only two channels in the 1970s, but they were priceless to us. Chairs, doors and windows had no value at all.

Denis and I had a chance to patch up our differences when we played hurling or football together. It took longer for Mary and I to find our peace. Happily, as we became adults, we also became good friends. She is married and living out in Watergrasshill now.

Outside the house I was always involved in some mischief or other. More often than not, Denis would be with me, leading the way most of the time. If there were a couple of horses in a field we would enjoy our own version of High Chaparral, a popular TV programme involving cowboys in the wild west, riding bareback. We would be joined in our adventures by friends like Philly, Pa and Dave Carroll, Tony and Derek Walsh, Martin and Patrick O'Keeffe, and Christy Cashman.

The horses were usually owned by Traveller families, and if we were caught we knew we would be in serious trouble. There were a couple of narrow escapes. If there were no horses around we would sometimes use cows as a substitute! It was wild and dangerous. Fortunately, no one got hurt.

Apart from the GAA pitch one of our favourite places of play was the Glashaboy River. We swam there and we often caught trout or salmon which we either brought home for dinner or gave out to our neighbours. Some of our pastimes were more legitimate. A man named John Kennelly – whose wife taught us in Brook Lodge school – would often ask us to come up to his farm and help pick potatoes. It was always the lads from Sarsfields that he asked. He paid us as well. The Kennelly's were always good to us, lovely people.

We picked tomatoes at Dooley's and more potatoes at Dunkettle House, so not all our time was spent getting into trouble. Denis claims, to this day, that I had a terrible temper. "You'd have had no friends at all if it wasn't for the GAA," he would tell me.

Even at that early age, hurling and football were the dominant themes in my life. Later, in my early teens, I did have another sporting outlet – soccer. There was no soccer in Glanmire at the time but, nearby in the city, the game was hugely popular. Part of my mother's weekly schedule was a Saturday morning visit to the hairdresser. She insisted that Denis and I would go with her. We would sit there for two hours aching to get out. She knew that if we were let loose we would probably cause some form of trouble.

The husband of the hairdresser was involved with a soccer club in Shandon and invited us along. We were delighted. Our only involvement with soccer up to then had been the games on The Green. Denis played outfield and it was immediately obvious that he had a talent for the game.

Very quickly, it was also established that I would be a goalkeeper. I was already getting a reputation in hurling and football for my ability in the air and this was recognised by the coaches in Shandon. When crosses or corners came into my area, I won every one of them.

We were playing Castle View Rovers one day. Daithi Downey, who was in school with me in North Mon, was playing for them. They were peppering our goal, whipping in crosses and taking shots. I saved them. They won a lot of corners. The ball would be aimed for Daithi's head. I would leap through the air and pluck every ball off the top of his head. "Christ lads, keep it away from him he's like an octopus," Daithi roared.

Soccer fitted into our schedule. In the city, under-age GAA games were played on Sunday mornings but, outside the city, in places like Glanmire, that did not happen because the times might clash with Mass times. You missed Mass at your peril when I was growing up. If, by chance, you did miss Mass you would always make it your business to find out the contents of the sermon in case you were quizzed later. There were some Sundays when my mother gave us her blessing to miss Mass if we had a soccer game. She was just happy that we were gainfully entertained.

I played for a few years and enjoyed it immensely. Denis and I played with some very good players, including the likes of Patsy Freyne who went to England for a while but spent most of his career with Cork City. But, as the demands on my time grew as I began to play hurling and football more seriously, I found I just did not have the time to keep it up. Hurling was my passion, and football existed side by side with that. There just wasn't room for soccer in my life.

At Brook Lodge and with Sarsfields I continued to make progress as a hurler and footballer. I was becoming well known around the East Cork area as a youngster with promise. There was another kid from Midleton who was being paired with me as two likely lads for the future. His name was Colm O'Neill. We would have many battles at club level in the years ahead and would become solid teammates with the Cork footballers.

I was nearing the end of my time in Brook Lodge. I approached that prospect with uncertainty. I enjoyed the school, if not the study, and I was unsure of the future. Denis was already working to bring in an income. What did the future hold for me? I wondered would I also be sent out to work. It wasn't something that I wanted to do even though all my older siblings had made that sacrifice. I just wanted to play hurling and football and that would not be as easy if I was working.

Once again, fortune smiled on me. My mother decided that I would continue with my education.

The big question was, where?

•••••

North Monastery is one of the oldest schools in Ireland with a tradition of academic achievement and a list of illustrious past pupils, that includes the name of Jack Lynch.

It was also a renowned hurling nursery. That made it the one and only secondary school that I would agree to attend. Therein lay a very big problem. There were various criteria for gaining entry to North Mon, as it was and still is known. The entrance exam was the most obvious starting point. I suspect my entrance exam was spectacular for all the wrong reasons. It was also a help if a sibling had attended the school. That didn't apply in my case.

So, with a little over a week to the start of the school year of 1978-79 I had failed to secure a place at North Mon and was stubbornly refusing to consider any other option. My poor mother had enough problems to deal with without a sulky thirteen-year-old refusing to go to school.

A good family friend, Sean Farrell, intervened. He was a past pupil of North Mon and a good friend of the principal at the time, a Brother Barry. Sean spoke to him and arranged for my mother and myself to go to meet him on the Wednesday morning before the new term began. I don't remember much about the meeting, except that I was nervous. Whatever was said – or I suspect whatever Sean had said beforehand – impressed Brother Barry. I was offered a place and signed the code of conduct. Included was a pledge to play for whatever teams on which you were selected. I went home that evening the happiest boy in Cork.

The following Monday morning, I stood at the bottom of the terrace waiting for the double-decker bus to stop in Glanmire and bring me into the city. It was packed from top to bottom and you could barely see your way with the amount of cigarette smoke in the air. Going into the city was an adventure for me. We went to the city only rarely and it was nearly always on a Saturday for a swim in the corporation baths beside City Hall.

I got off at Parnell Place and walked across to Patrick Street to get the No. 2 bus that brought me up to the Mon. I was amazed at the crowds of people on the move at that time of the day. That first journey to school was like a trip to Dublin. It was a complete change of scenery, and different pace of life. Our walks to Brook Lodge National School or anywhere around Glanmire were sedate, peaceful events. This was madness, with people rushing here and there, no one talking to anyone else, no one recognising anyone else. No one made eye contact; all were intent on getting to their destination on time.

Between the primary and secondary schools in North Mon, there must have been 1,200 boys converging on the school at the same time. It was intimidating, exciting and frightening all at once. I didn't know anyone and I certainly felt a bit self-conscious going there for the first time. City boys were much more confident. I was like all lads from outside the city, quiet and a bit unsure of myself. I had to learn fairly quickly to stand up for myself, to establish a presence and gain the respect of my peers. That's where the hurling field became my place.

The Christian Brothers, who ran North Monastery at the time, prioritised academia. They lectured us on day one about the importance of education and achieving the best results possible in all examinations. I was no Einstein, not by a long shot, and that ethos might have terrified me. But there was another priority in the Mon and that was hurling. There were men at the school, brothers and lay teachers, who were fanatical about the game. They were so proud of the school's history on the hurling fields and the Harty Cup – the Munster colleges senior hurling championship – would have been described as a second religion if such a description was not regarded as sacrilegious.

I had often heard stories of the Harty Cup when I was growing up, from men like Mickey Barry and Bertie Murphy. Tadhg Murphy, Bertie's son, had a brilliant Harty Cup career and that had been an inspiration to me. Those stories had fed my desire to one day attend North Mon. I had no great interest or ambition on the academic side but I was prepared to make the effort if it gave me the opportunity to play hurling.

From day one, I was hooked on the traditions and importance of the Harty Cup. My talent was spotted immediately. I remember the first long walk up Church Street, up Fair Hill with my hurley, kit bag and school bag full of books to the school sports grounds. Brother Gibson was a fanatical hurling man, a member of the Glen Rovers club, who had been involved in many of the school's successes and he took me under his wing, encouraging me and giving me the confidence to express myself on the field.

During my early days on those fields I first met Murt Murphy, a teacher at North Mon, who would have a major influence on my development as a person and as a hurler. It was he who introduced me to the need for tactical awareness. He taught me about structure and technique, how to make the best of my individual talents within a team environment.

Murt helped in many ways. In an effort to bring some money into the house, I worked every Saturday with Pat Fahy, a plasterer who was originally from Galway. Pat paid me £10 for the day. But, at North Mon, we were expected to train on Saturdays. I told Murt I couldn't train because I could not afford to be without the money. Murt made sure that if I missed work to go training I would get the £10 anyway.

It wasn't all plain sailing. I hit one very rocky patch during my second year in the school. We had a new principal, a Brother Burke, and he was a tough, no-holds-barred type of man. We didn't get along and I gave him ammunition to have a go at me. As I've explained, on entering North Mon all boys agreed to make themselves available to play for whatever team selected them. Breach of that agreement could lead to expulsion. Typically, stubborn Teddy flirted with disaster.

One Friday afternoon, early in second year, I decided that I wanted to enjoy the good autumn weather at home. We had a game that afternoon against St Colman's College of Fermoy. If I had told someone that I was injured or that there was some problem at home that would prevent me from playing, my absence wouldn't have really mattered. But I just packed up my things and got the bus home. I thought no more about it that weekend.

On the Monday morning in science class, I noted the arrival of the principal. He didn't speak to me but, when he left, the teacher told me to go the principal's office. I went in trepidation.

When he confronted me I had no excuse to offer, and he threatened to impose the most serious sanction. I couldn't believe it. This was the school I had so desperately wanted to attend; I had enjoyed my first year and was looking forward to a good second year, and now I had put all that in jeopardy. What was I going to tell my mother?

It took a lot of negotiation – I always believed Murt Murphy worked very hard on my behalf behind the scenes – before the principal relented and I was allowed to continue as a pupil. I never missed a game again.

It was during that second year that I got my first small taste of Harty Cup hurling. Though very young, I was asked to go along for Harty trials. It was very unusual for a second year to be asked, so there was a fair bit of attention on me. I felt like a boy going in against men. But I had had a good education back in Sarsfields, and in East Cork juvenile games, by that stage. I wasn't afraid of bigger men. In fact, I loved playing alongside lads with so much skill. Tony O'Sullivan and Tomas Mulcahy had broken through by then and were some of the main players for the school that year. I enjoyed the intensity of the hurling, the speed with which the ball was moved.

At the back of my mind I realised that I would be too young to be included on the Harty panel but I was determined to make a good impression. They told me that I did, and I watched with satisfaction as the team went on to win the Harty Cup and the All-Ireland title, in 1980.

It was around that time that Murt Murphy and a young teacher at the school, Donal O'Grady, took me aside and told me it was time to change my grip. I was almost fifteen years old and completely taken aback. It had never really occurred to me that I was using an unorthodox left hand over right grip on the stick, the golfer's grip rather than the accepted right over left. I trusted them and was prepared to spend an extra hour in the evenings in the handball alley, belting the ball against the wall and getting used to the new grip. I can only describe it as like being asked to start writing with your right hand after using your left for thirteen years.

The benefits became apparent in the school year of 1980-81. I established myself as a regular on the Harty Cup team, playing at left half-forward. It became almost the entire focus of the year. You were treated differently as a student. A Harty Cup player was a god-like figure in the school. He was given preferential treatment and made to feel special and, from time to time, the Harty player was allowed to skip classes to attend team meetings.

Two mornings a week, at break, the canteen would be cleared of all other students at 10.20am. Even if they hadn't finished whatever they had brought to school to eat, they were hustled out of the canteen and we were brought in, to be fed soup and sandwiches, and have a discussion about whatever game lay ahead that week. From two biscuits handed out by Ellen to this! I had it made.

On the day of a game the city boys would be allowed to go home early to get something to eat while the country lads, like myself, would be brought up to the Brothers' house. The food served there was as good as you would get in the best hotel in Cork. It was an eerie feeling to be sitting in the same room as all these men with their black robes and white collars. But the quality of the food overcame our fears and queasiness.

I recall one memorable occasion, when, for a few of us 'culchies', it was not possible to be fed in the big house. It was decided, instead, that John O'Neill, Kieran Horgan, Michael Drinan and I would be allowed to dine at the Uptown Grill on McCurtain Street. Murt gave us a blank cheque and the restaurant was informed that we were to be looked after. I'm sure Murt and the Brothers expected four young lads to order chicken and chips, or something like that. We had other ideas.

The four of us ordered the biggest steaks we could get. That was after our starters. We finished up with the best desserts the Uptown Grill could provide. We had a mighty feast. I can only imagine what the Brothers and Murt thought when the bill came up on the bank statement. It was never mentioned. Cost was not an issue when it came to preparing for the Harty Cup.

We were well kitted out. Coming from our clubs, where money was always tight and where you might have one yellow sock and one red one, where nothing but the jersey was coordinated, here the uniform was perfect.

My first year of Harty Cup hurling in 1980-81 was my most successful. We won the cup that year, beating Colaiste Chriost Ri in an all-Cork final in Pairc Ui Chaoimh. They were better known as a football school and were completely dominant in Munster at the time, winning a third consecutive Munster senior football title that year. Many of the same players were on the hurling team and, at half time in the final, they probably thought they would do the double that year. They had played much better than us and were leading.

Robbie Allen was playing in his second Harty Cup final. He was one of our best players but was having a difficult day in the final. Tony Leahy was brilliant for Chriost Ri at midfield. He cleaned us out and was winning the Harty Cup almost on his own. But, at the start of the second half, Robbie and Tony were involved in an altercation. Both were sent off. Losing Robbie would normally have been a disaster for us. But on the day Tony was a much bigger loss to Chriost Ri. We turned the game around, and I won a Harty Cup medal at the first attempt.

Although we beat Our Lady's of Gort easily enough in the All-Ireland semi-final we were surprisingly beaten in the final, by Kilkenny CBS, in Walsh Park in Waterford. They scored a freakish goal that day from a free. A lad named Tom Bawle took it. It must have been 90 yards from our goal. The ball sailed all the way to the net without anyone touching it. It was that school's only All-Ireland Colleges title at senior level.

The Harty Cup was an amazing competition and experience. It dominated our lives and prepared us for the future. To get to a final was a special event. In North Mon the students would compile a magazine for the game with pen pictures of the players, articles about the history of the competition and interviews.

Twenty 52-seater buses would leave the school on the day of the game. Crowds flocked to the games and we played in front of 5,000 to 6,000 spectators.

Although I did not win another Harty Cup during my time in North Mon, the competition sustained me through my years at the school. We got to the final the following year and were beaten by St Flannan's from Ennis. They would be our nemesis. I was appointed captain of the school team for the 1982-83 season. We reached the final again, and again St Flannan's were our opponents. I probably played my best game for Mon in the drawn game but the lads up front had a frustrating day. Kieran Horgan and John O'Neill did everything but put the ball over the bar. They hit the crossbar, they hit the upright. The ball just wouldn't go over.

Even still, we were a point ahead near the end when they got an equalising point. Flannan's won the replay by two points. We scored just one point in the first half that day but thundered into the game in the second half. We had left ourselves too much to do. It was the worst experience of my life in sport at the time.

Compared to other events in my life at the time, however, it was insignificant.

CHAPTER**4**

MOTHERLY LOVE

St Finbarr's Hospital stands on the Douglas Road in Cork. It has been Ellen's home for the past 32 years. She lies there in a vegetative state, barely able to communicate.

I don't go to see her very often. Don't expect me to offer any excuses for that. It is not something that is easy to rationalise. It just breaks my heart to see someone I had such a close relationship with lying there, being fed intravenously.

Ellen was 21 years old on March 30 in 1980. She hadn't any big celebration planned. In fact, if memory serves me right, she was going to stay at home in Glanmire that evening to have a small party with us. A friend called at one stage in the evening and suggested they head out for a celebratory drink. Ellen couldn't decide whether to go or not. My mother encouraged her. Ellen worked hard outside the home, and in the home. She deserved a night out.

They were driving over a rise in the road out near Ballyvolane. A lorry was parked on the side of the road. The car, in which Ellen was the front seat passenger, ploughed into the lorry. The extent of the impact was such that the engine of the lorry actually started.

Ellen was thrown out through the windscreen. She was almost decapitated. When the emergency services arrived on the scene they did not expect her to live. My mother and the older members of the family rushed to her bedside, and they were quickly told that it was very unlikely she would survive the night such was the extent of the injuries to her head. She was put on a life support machine, and we all just waited and prayed.

Friends and relations, like Fr Keane from West Cork and a cousin, Richie Barry, provided comfort and support. My mother had dealt with tragedy before in her life but this was the first time that I recognised how stricken she was with grief. On top of everything else that life had thrown at her this was completely shattering.

The doctors had done everything they could. At an early stage they told us that Ellen was gone; only the machine was keeping her alive. They advised my mother that she should consent to the machine being turned off and that Ellen should be allowed to die. Looking back, I think that even at fifteeen years of age I realised it was probably the right thing to do. Everyone was telling my mother to agree, but she wouldn't.

Maybe she couldn't bear the thought of losing another child. She and Ellen had been great friends, they were always messing about in the kitchen, joking and laughing, and they were more like sisters or very close friends than mother and daughter. She couldn't bear to let go. It was a horrible place for my mother to be in. How could a parent agree to end the life of a child?

Sometimes I wonder about this thing called a sixth sense. I don't generally believe in such things. But my mother held on to a slim hope that Ellen would recover, and she delayed a decision on the machine as long as she could before relenting after three weeks.

They turned off the machine and Ellen continued to breathe.

In the days and weeks since the accident she had recovered sufficiently to breathe on her own. She would remain dependant for the rest of her life, but she was breathing. If my mother had not been so determined then Ellen would surely have passed on.

In the early days when she was moved to St Finbarr's, I did visit her. Here was this fine, athletic, talented, lively, outdoor-type girl who had been so full of life and gave so much of herself to her family, and to me especially, now lying unmoving on a bed. I hated looking at her in that state. I found it shattering. Eventually I stopped going to see her.

Thinking about it – not going to see her – constantly upsets me. We were so close and I think that is the root of the problem. It was after seeing her that I had real problems. I wouldn't be the better for it for days. It made me very unhappy and I was difficult to be around.

I do go in for special occasions. We went in for photographs on the day I got married, but I always find it so hard, and it hasn't got any easier over the years. Even this year when Ellen was unwell at the start of the summer and we thought she might pass on I went to see her, but I found it so difficult.

Coming out of the hospital I feel broken. I know that is a poor excuse but it is the way I am. Just reading those words I feel I am being selfish but I want to remember Ellen the way she was when she was well and we would be out in the garden hurling away and having fun, playing the sport we both loved so much.

The rest of the family are brilliant with Ellen. One day might go past without someone dropping in but not two. They have developed a form of communication. They ask questions about her childhood and they get a response, one word and maybe another, and they ask her some simple addition and she mouths an answer.

I often wonder how Ellen would have reacted to my success on hurling and football fields. I think she would have enjoyed it more than anyone but she would never have let me know. That was the way she was. She never allowed you to think you were better than anyone else. She kept my teenage feet firmly planted on the ground even when others were telling me what a talent I had.

Over the coming years, Ellen couldn't be with me but her influence always remained. Until the day my mother died, in 2009, I don't think she ever got over Ellen's accident. It was only during that period in 1980 that I began to realise the effects these tragedies had on her. It brought us closer together as a family and Ellen's brothers and sisters all got on with life, but I don't think my mother ever came to terms with that tragedy.

Peter Holland had fought his tumour bravely. He was a tower of strength when Ellen had her accident. But Peter's battle ended on November 24, 1981. Breda lost a husband, the two girls lost a father and the rest of us lost a valuable friend.

•••••

My mother didn't display affection in a grand manner. She wasn't loud or demonstrative, and she didn't have the time or the inclination to constantly remind us that she loved us. So much was happening through her life that I would be surprised if she ever had time to compartmentalise her emotions. Life was not easy and I didn't make it any easier as a child. As the years passed and I got older, I did begin to notice her attention. It was subtle and unpronounced but it was also obvious. The rest of the family noticed as well. It was obvious from an early stage, though I did not admit it for years, that I was her pet.

It manifested itself first in the way she protected me from outraged parents of children to whom I might have administered some unfair punishment for a perceived insult. Denis would never have got away with some of the things that I did. I did get a lash from time to time and always deserved it, but I also knew that I was safe in her presence even when I didn't deserve to be.

Whenever I was in trouble she would make an excuse for me. "Sure, God love him, he had a hard time growing up," she would say.

She was a humble person and she passed on that humility to us. But she was also proud. In the early days after my father died we might not have had food on the table but when we left for school or Mass or games, we were properly turned out. I could be gasping for a drink and not have the price of one but I would be the best turned out person on the street.

Our clothes were always clean and pressed. We were clean. And no matter how dirty we might get playing in the fields, in the garden or on The Green, by the following morning we were presentable again.

Sunday was her special day. She might have worked the late shift on Saturday and would not have got to bed until the early hours of the morning, but she would be up bright and early on a Sunday morning preparing a family dinner. No matter how tight her budget was she would always have enough to provide a roast of beef or lamb or pork for the extended family for Sunday. I remember those gatherings as real feasts. All of her children would gather and, as the years went by, they would bring husbands, wives and their children. The food was fantastic. It was like Christmas Day every

Sunday. When lunch was over we would all head outside to the garden and play hurling for an hour or two.

Mam's only role then would be to patch up whatever part of the various bodies would be split open in the exchanges. Very often even she couldn't stem the flow of blood, and one or other of us would have to go to the doctor or the hospital the following day to have a few stitches inserted.

The numbers who came for Sunday lunch continued to grow, over the years.

Pat and his wife Grace, who sadly died from cancer, had five children – Carmel, Brian, Robert, Alan and Laura. Breda and Peter's daughters Michelle and Deirdre were always around, especially after Peter died in 1981. Breda later remarried to Ger Gray and they have one son, Gary.

Philly and her husband, Benny Jenkinson, have two daughters, Leslie and Helena. Denis, would you believe it, went into enemy territory and married an Erin's Own girl, Mary. They have a daughter, Shona, and son, Donncha. Our own Mary married Dermot Sullivan, a man with Kerry blood in him, they have a son, Keelan, and a daughter, Elle.

Oonagh and I added to the gathering. Cian was the first-born, followed by Niall, in 1992, and then Sinead, who was 13 years old in April, 2012.

The only thing that impacted on those early Sunday gatherings was my involvement in hurling and football. As a kid all our games were played on a Saturday but, as I got older and began to play with more teams, I seemed to have a match nearly every Sunday. The time of my game dictated the time for lunch.

By the time I was 14 or 15, I was playing or training every night of the week. I would play at different age levels for Sarsfields and Glanmire. When I was 15, I was playing Under-21 hurling for Sarsfields. I was only 16 when I played senior hurling with the club and played intermediate football with Glanmire. Then I began to be selected on under-age squads for Cork. The demands on my time and energy were heavy but I had no problem with that. I loved what I was doing. There was also a heavy demand on gear. That was Mam's problem and she never complained.

What she did was incredible. At one stage I was playing for nine different teams. In a two-week period in August of 1982, I played six Championship games in twelve days! We won the East Cork minor Championship double that year. I had just turned 17. We didn't have a washing machine in the house so everything had to be washed by hand. Before she went to work or after she got home she would gather the dirty gear and start scrubbing. Remember what the gear was like then, heavy woollen jerseys, heavy togs that picked up grass stains which were almost impossible to remove. My mother removed them. Her knuckles would be raw from scrubbing. My togs were always pristine white.

She would work out my schedule, which team I was training with or playing with. I never had to worry about putting my gear together. The bag would be left in the kitchen for me and I wouldn't have to check it. No matter which team I was playing for, she would have the right gear prepared. It came home covered in muck and shite, but when I saw it again the next time it would be gleaming.

I was the best-dressed hurler and footballer, not just in Glanmire and East Cork. I was the best turned out in all of Cork. My knicks would be ironed with a perfect crease. Even my socks were ironed.

She never talked much about hurling or football. She would always ask about results and she was very encouraging. From time to time, I would be aware that people would be talking about me and whatever success I was having, but she never mentioned it. But I knew she was happy and proud. She showed that by the way she prepared everything for me. It was her contribution to my success, her way of saying well done.

As I got older and started playing in big club games on Sundays, the family lunch was timed to suit me. She knew my routine. If the game was to be played in the evening I started the day by buying the Sunday newspapers and then going to Mass. I liked to eat around the middle of the day so everyone would have to be at the house ready to eat at 12noon. Then I would get a few hours sleep before playing the game. If noon did not suit someone, she would quietly explain, "Teddy has a match."

I might come home from school or later on from work and she would know I was training in the evening. My bag would be ready for me. I would have a sandwich and go into the front room for a rest for an hour. We only had the two rooms, the kitchen and the front room. Once I fell asleep the front room was out of bounds to everyone else. Denis and Mary were barred until I woke.

"Don't wake him," she would warn them in a tone that allowed for no argument. Of course, I would wake as cranky as hell and showed no appreciation at all for their sacrifice.

Amidst all the hardship and tragedy in her life I think my success was a welcome diversion. She stopped going to games when I started playing really seriously, at around the age of 18 or 19. But she often travelled to somewhere like Killarney or Dublin and would window-shop while the game was on before meeting the rest of the family after the game when she would enquire how I got on.

She wasn't completely blind to my faults and was not slow to correct me when she felt I had done wrong. But there is no question I got off lightly.

I should recount one story to explain. Denis and I shared a bedroom at the back of the house. It had two beds, a double underneath the window and a single in which I slept. Being older and earning an income, Denis became involved in the social scene a while before I did. The social scene then, of course, was drinking. My mother didn't approve but she couldn't control all of us all the time.

Anyway, the first night I ventured into the social world that was the local woods where we consumed cans of beer and whatever other concoction youngsters could find, my mother was working the late shift. She assumed that Denis would be going out for the night and that I would be in bed early, in preparation for a game on the Sunday morning.

The truth was that Denis was working and had come home early, tired and sleepy. He was in bed and in a deep slumber by the time I got home, full to the gills and struggling with the unfamiliar taste of alcohol on my tongue. My stomach was rumbling before I lay down and I realised I was going to be sick. The toilet was downstairs and I knew I would not make it. The only other possible place for me to deposit the contents of my stomach was out the window, underneath which Denis was snoring.

I didn't make it across the room. I began to throw up from my side of the room and continued across to Denis's bed. I got sick on his bed before I got to the window. I covered the sill and the vomit dropped to the ground below outside the kitchen window.

Before getting into bed I cleaned up as best I could. But I couldn't clean up where Denis was sleeping in case I woke him.

At 9am the following morning my mother came in to wake us for Mass. The first thing that hit her was the smell. Then she looked around the room. My bed was clean. There were sick stains around Denis's bed clothing and on the window-sill.

"Jesus Christy almighty, what happened here?" she shouted.

She bent down to pick up one of Denis's shoes and proceeded to whack him across the shoulders. "What in God's name were you up to last night?" she demanded.

Denis woke up with a fright.

"What is it?" he asked.

When he looked around him he copped on. "It wasn't me, I wasn't drinking at all last night. I wasn't out. It must have been Teddy."

She whacked him doubly hard.

"That's terrible to be blaming someone else. Sure, Teddy doesn't drink at all." I eventually told her the truth many, many years later when I was best man at Denis's wedding. That was my mother. She didn't display her affection or her pride with words or gestures. She did it with motherly actions that I only appreciated as I got older.

•••••

Between the school and the club I was always playing hurling and, to a slightly lesser extent, football. I had passed Mickey Barry's tutelage by the age of 13 when men like Timmy Walsh and Diarmuid 'Dermy' Kelleher took us over. Sarsfields hadn't enjoyed a great deal of success prior to this at under-age level. They were bigger clubs like Midleton and Carrigtwohill that would be too strong for smaller clubs like Sarsfields.

I came along at a good time. John Considine, who would later play alongside me with Cork, was also emerging and we began to enjoy a lot of success. Initially, we played most of our hurling and football around East Cork but, as we began to move up the divisions, our playing area expanded to include the west. That was good for me because no one over there had heard of me. In East Cork I was a marked man. In Skibbereen they didn't know who I was and that gave me freedom from the sort of attention that was my lot in the east of the county.

There was one particular game at Under-16 level, the first round of the East Cork Championship against Carrigtwohill, that was memorable for the attention I received. I was not even 14 at the time and playing at midfield. Denis was centre half-back. I was taking a lot of punishment from my marker and at one stage retaliated. Minutes later he got his revenge. He nearly took my head off. I was getting treatment when all hell broke loose on the field. Denis had sought retribution and a big row broke out.

The game was abandoned.

After an investigation by the Cork County GAA Board, during which Mickey Barry tried to use all his powers of persuasion, Denis was suspended for twelve months. My name wasn't mentioned in connection with the incident.

I was just fifteen years old when I played Under-21 Championship hurling with Sarsfields. Just a year later I played with the club's senior hurlers for the first time. We were graded as an intermediate football club at the time and, in that same year, 1982, I played with the Glanmire adults for the first time. I was very young but I don't ever remember being intimidated by playing against grown men. All my experiences at school and with the club had me well prepared. That was the year when I first came to the attention of the Cork selectors, although I didn't enjoy a very successful start.

Early that year, I had been invited to trials for the Cork minor football team. I went along on a couple of occasions and felt I was doing okay. The numbers were reduced each time and when it came down to the final 40 I thought I had a decent chance of making the final squad. Then it all went quiet. I heard nothing more. I was in school towards the end of April when I heard a couple of the lads talking about the minors.

"What's going on?" I enquired, to be told they had beaten Tipperary in the first round of the Munster Championship. All the talk was of Colm O'Neill who had scored two goals. A month later they beat Limerick in the Munster semi-final. "That's it, no minor football for me this year," I thought and consoled myself with the prospect that my form for North Mon and for Sarsfields might earn me selection with the minor hurlers.

One Saturday evening as the summer began, I was playing for Glanmire in an intermediate football League game. Shamrocks were the opposition. My brother, Pat, had joined the club when he moved to South Cork and was involved that evening. I had heard himself and his friends talking in the past about this crack midfielder they had. I was marking him and cleaned him out. The Shamrocks manager was a man named Neilly Mahony. He spoke to Pat.

"What age is that brother of yours?"

"He'll be 17 in July," Pat Told him.

"Then why isn't he on the Cork minor team?"

Neilly knew most of the people involved in Cork football. He had heard stories about the minor team that year. The word was that it wasn't a great team. "If your brother can't make at least the subs then there's something wrong," he told Pat, and promised to do something about it. A few days later I got a message to turn up for a trial game. A Cork minor selection would play the Nemo Rangers Under-21 team. I was selected at full-forward and suffered a miserable first half hour in a role I had never played before. I was always a midfielder with a roving role and I was like a duck out of water in the full-forward line.

They persisted with me for the second half, but they released me to centre half-forward. There I was marked by Jimmy Kerrigan, a man I would get to know very well in the years to come. We had a good battle and I eventually began to show what I could do. I scored a goal and two points in the second half. A friend of mine, Brendan Lotty, came on for the second half and scored 1-4. At the end of the game, after we had changed, Brendan and I sat together as the panel to attend training the following Tuesday night was called out. My name was included, Brendan's wasn't. I couldn't work that one out. He had played well and scored more than me. But I was chosen.

We played Kerry in the Munster final in Pairc Ui Chaoimh on July 4, 1982. I was given the No.20 jersey, and I was brought on in the second half as a midfield replacement for Brendan Stack from Doneraile. Kerry beat us 1-11 to 0-5.

Our local newspaper, *The Southern Star*, had praise for my contribution but also reflected a general view of the team. The reporter Noel Horgan wrote: "Cork introduced Teddy McCarthy at midfield and he made a definite impact, performing with more drive and determination than any of the first-choice fifteen. However, he could do little to stem the tide as Kerry's greater balance was vital and the visitors effortlessly maintained their edge to the end.

"Mick Maguire, John Quilter, Kieran McCarthy, Colm O'Neill and Teddy McCarthy were the few players who looked equipped to compete at this level on the most inept Cork minor team for years."

I had jumped for a couple of balls with Sean Wight, their No. 9. I was good at getting off the ground and he was just as good. It was no surprise he went on to make a career for himself in Australian Rules football. It is hard to believe he is no longer with us. Another good player on that Kerry team was Michael McAuliffe.

We had some decent footballers ourselves, lads that I would get to know much better as the years went on and who would enjoy better days in Killarney. In the squad were Denis Walsh, Michael Slocum, Barry Coffey, Tony Davis and Michael McCarthy.

I was now beginning to attract some attention. Glanmire reached the final of the Cork county minor Championship. We lost to St Finbarr's by just four points. The local newspaper eulogised: "As a promising young footballer, McCarthy was a revelation at midfield, an oasis in a desert of mediocrity and, though the general standard of play was unimpressive on Sunday, the Glanmire lad indicated quite clearly that there is at least one budding football talent in the county. McCarthy took some hard knocks in the second half but, true sportsman that he is, he accepted it all and got on with the play. His impeccable high fielding and expertly placed passes were straight out of Declan Barron's copybook and his ability to move from one end of the field to the other was reminiscent of Pat Spillane at his best."

It was good to read such praise but I stayed grounded. My mother ensured that I did. Denis and Pat would also make sure that I didn't get too cocky. Confidence was important but I was never allowed to think I was untouchable.

I was also involved with the county minor hurlers that summer, but it was uneventful. Cork lost to Tipperary in the first round by just one point. It was the prelude to an under-age hurling career with Cork that took in the minor and under-21 grades and would be one of the least distinguished periods in the history of Cork hurling. You would think being born in Cork would be a massive advantage for any young hurler. Well, between minor and Under-21, I played for five seasons and won a total of two games. Both of those were at Under-21 level and against Waterford, in 1983 and 1986. I didn't even get my place on the team in '83!

I was involved in two minor Championship games – Tipperary beat us in the first round in 1982 when I did not get my place; we lost to Limerick in the first round in 1983 and I'm glad to say I played well. It did give me more time to dedicate to my club, my divisional football team and my other football commitments. Fortunately, I was enjoying a lot more success with the bigger ball.

•••••

I ran onto Croke Park for the first time as a Cork player in the early afternoon of August 21, 1983. I was a minor footballer and we were the Munster champions playing Kildare in the All-Ireland semi-final. Strangely, I remember more about the senior game that day. Our seniors played Dublin and it was a dramatic game that ended in a draw.

We beat Kildare in a tight game. I was the free-taker that year and kicked a few of them in the semi-final. One of those was kicked into Hill 16. It was rapidly filling up with the colourful Dublin supporters and they were favouring Kildare in the minor game. As I lined up the free, I could hear the catcalls increasing in intensity. When the ball went over the bar I stuck two fingers up to the Hill. It was my first act of defiance in Croke Park.

The year had begun in the middle of May. The draw for the Championship pitted us against Kerry in the first round. It was played in Kilmallock and we won comfortably. We then beat Clare and Tipperary to win the Munster Championship. Now we had reached the All-Ireland final and would meet a good Derry team who had one of the outstanding under-age footballers of our generation, Dermot McNicholl, in their forward line. I would get to know Dermot well in the years to come.

Our final is forgotten now. It was the curtain-raiser to a senior final that remains notorious in the history of football. Four players were sent off, three from Dublin, as they bravely won the All-Ireland title against Galway. It was a horrible day for football and that game was as rancorous as any final I have seen since. Our game was timid in comparison. Derry won by 0-8 to 1-3, the low scoring a testament to the conditions.

Losing was a disappointment but the blow was absorbed by the entire experience. Here we were, a disparate bunch of youngsters from all parts of Cork spending two nights in a swanky Dublin hotel, mixing with our heroes on the senior football team. On the day after the game the four teams were brought together for a reception at The Burlington Hotel, where we were staying.

The Dublin legend, Brian Mullins, had been sent off in the senior final. There were rumours of fighting in the tunnel at half time involving Galway's Brian Talty. When the two men met in the foyer of the hotel on Monday everyone expected something like the Gunfight at the O.K. Corral. A bunch of us followed them around the hotel and outside as they tried to get some privacy. It became comical, like one of those silent movies where everyone kept following everyone else, ducking in and out of doorways.

At least we thought it was great fun. I'd say the two lads would have lynched us if they had got their hands on us. They just wanted to find a quiet spot where they could sort everything out between them.

That final was the beginning of a journey for me. From that day until the end of 1990 I would complete every year by playing in an All-Ireland final in either football or hurling. And I didn't know it then, but I would win a lot more than I would lose, at the end of it all creating a special piece of GAA history.

CHAPTER**5**

COMING OF AGE

Ireland in the mid-1980s was an awful lot like it is today, deep in recession, but I don't remember people being as gloomy as they are now.

We did have unemployment, emigration, factory closures and industrial strife. There weren't as many opportunities for furthering your education after school as there are today, although that wouldn't have mattered to me anyway. Once I left North Mon with my Leaving Certificate completed I had no intention of spending any more time on study.

That did present me with a problem. I needed a job and there weren't any available. Young people my age were leaving Ireland every week in search of employment. Young Irish voices echoed around the big cities of England, in London, Liverpool, Birmingham and Manchester.

Many others were heading for the usual destinations in North America. I knew fellas my age who had gone to New York, Boston, Chicago and San Francisco. The GAA clubs in those cities were busy recruiting young footballers and hurlers, promising them summer jobs if they went over and played for their teams.

Emigration was a way of life for most families in Cork, and throughout Ireland. Members of my father's family had gone abroad, as had many of my mother's siblings. My father and mother, too, had planned life outside Ireland but fate decreed they should stay. My brother Michael had gone and died abroad. Pat had also spent a short time in England.

I had been so absorbed in my sporting activities that I hadn't given a lot of thought to seeking permanent employment until the beginning of 1984. I had worked at a few part-time jobs since I was thirteen years old but, now, I needed to think in the long term. And the fact that I was a promising hurler and footballer didn't initially open any doors.

From Monday to Friday my evenings were busy. And no weekend passed without being involved in at least one and, very often, two games. But my days were empty. I was like tens of thousands of others searching the 'Situations Vacant' columns in the newspaper and hoping that something would turn up.

A number of contemporaries from Glanmire had already left for America. My commitments to the club and to Cork had stopped me from contemplating such a move, however, by the end of the spring of 1984 I had a change of mind and heart. I told my mother that I would be going to America for the summer at least, and possibly longer if the opportunity arose. While Ireland was in recession there was nothing in the country for me.

The word spread.

Some people in Sarsfields spoke to me and asked me to wait until they explored the possibility of finding me a job. Jim Darcy, a member of the club, came to me one evening. He was the Head Brewer with Beamish & Crawford, one of the biggest businesses in Cork, and said that there might be a job with the company for the summer months when they traditionally took on temporary staff to cope with extra demand. He was true to his word.

I postponed my departure to America. Beamish & Crawford was a welcoming environment and I liked it immediately. The job was temporary but I felt like I belonged. While the brewery was busy during the summer months there was plenty of work. At the end of September I was told there would be more work during the Christmas period. I went back then and was later made permanent.

In making the decision to go to America I hadn't given a lot of thought to the impact it would have on my sporting pursuits. I didn't have the arrogance to think that I would automatically become a senior footballer or hurler with Cork. I had hoped it would happen, of course, and was ambitious. But I needed a job and that was the priority. If Jim Darcy and Beamish & Crawford had not intervened, who knows if I would ever had played for the county and gone on to enjoy success.

My new job meant that in 1984, the Centenary Year of the GAA, I was living and breathing Gaelic Games.

I played for nine teams that year – Sarsfields Under-21 and senior hurling, Cork Under-21 hurling, Glanmire Under-21 and intermediate football, Cork Under-21, junior and senior football, as well as playing with the Divisional football team, Imokilly, that was made up of players from the intermediate and junior clubs in the area to play in the Cork senior Championship. Between training and playing I was on the go the whole time. I had no time for a social life, and no time to get into trouble.

My involvement with the Cork senior footballers was restricted. At the start of the year I was brought into the training panel. Joe McGrath was coaching Cork at the time and he used me in a couple of Tournament games and League games. I trained with them for the Championship but only got on the bench for the Munster final against Kerry when John Cleary had to pull out with an injury. Barry Coffey got a goal that day when he came on as a substitute and I remember thinking that I would love to have got a chance.

Barry and I had other things on our minds that Sunday in early July. We were training together with the Cork Under-21 footballers. Bob Honohan was our coach and we sensed from early meetings that he had assembled a decent squad of players. We were two of the 1983 minors promoted, so, too, were Michael Slocum and Mick McCarthy. Niall Cahalane was already established as a senior. We had Tony Davis, Tony Nation, a youngster with an American accent called Danny Culloty, Tony Leahy, Tom Mannix and Colm O'Neill. With that sort of talent it was no wonder that we blitzed both Clare and Limerick in the Munster Championship. We then beat Down in the All-Ireland semi-final.

Mayo, always under-age specialists at that time, were our opponents in the All-Ireland Under-21 final. They were the reigning champions and retained a number of their players from the previous year, like their goalkeeper Gabriel Irwin, John Finn, Padraig Brogan, Sean Maher, Noel Durkin and a big lad named Liam McHale. There were a lot of good footballers togging out in Ennis on August 27, but we didn't put on much of an exhibition.

We won by 0-9 to 0-6 and didn't care that it was a poor game. In less than a year, Bob had turned us into a tight-knit group. We were a young team, many of us eligible for the following year and a decent group of us who would be able to play again in 1986. Bob sowed sowed the seed of ambition before we broke up. Our target for 1985 was another Under-21 Championship title.

With the Under-21 Championship completed in '84 my season was still hectic. I always enjoyed playing with Imokilly. We had some really good footballers. The problem was that we were committed to our clubs first, and only really concentrated on the Divisional team when our clubs were eliminated from their respective competitions.

Lads like Denis Mulcahy and Kevin Hennessy from Midleton were well known as hurlers. Denis Walsh was already a regular teammate of mine on hurling and football teams and he played with Imokilly, as well. Conor Counihan was our captain and was already well known as a footballer. But there were others not as well known who were really talented, like Mattie Murphy from Youghal and Kieran Murphy from Castlemartyr. Kieran was only about five foot four but he was a real tiger, a great player. Four of us from Glanmire played, myself, Brian Lotty, Bertie Og and Tadhg Murphy. Bertie Murphy Snr was a selector. He was 76 at the time and as enthusiastic as a youngster. Dave Loughman coached us and did a great job.

As the season went on we built momentum. Dave was able to get us together for extra sessions and that helped make a team of us. We had two fairly easy wins against Bishopstown and Naomh Aban, before we needed a replay to beat UCC. We beat Duhallow in the semi-final but were still outsiders for the final against St Finbarr's. They had already won the Cork hurling title and were looking for a double. We beat them by four points in a huge upset. It was the perfect end to a good year.

I almost forgot: I also won an All-Ireland junior football Championship with Cork. We beat Wexford in the 'home' final and I scored two points. The team went on to play Warwickshire in the 'away' final and won that game without me.

If there was a disappointment that year it was defeat in the Munster Under-21 hurling Championship to Clare. John Barry and I were the two Sarsfields players on that team. I scored five points. Christy Ring Jnr played that day and scored four points.

There were loads of talented players in that squad, like Denis Walsh, Brendan O'Sullivan, Kieran Kingston, Ger Fitzgerald and Tomas Mulcahy. Tomas had already established himself with the Cork seniors and won his first All-Ireland title with them later in 1984. But we made no impact at all on the Championship in those years.

•••••

As Cork bathed in the glory of winning the Centenary All-Ireland hurling Championship I was amongst many past pupils invited back to North Mon when the Liam McCarthy Cup was brought to the school, in late September of '84. Many of the victorious team were past pupils and our former teacher and coach, Donal O'Grady was full-back.

Justin McCarthy had coached the team. An All-Ireland winner himself as a player, Justin was a well-respected coach by then, and shared the duties in Cork with Fr Michael O'Brien. I met Justin that day and we talked briefly about Cork's victory. "It could be you next year," he said, or words to that effect.

I thought about it. Since I was a young kid I had dreamed of playing for the Cork hurlers. Now, even after what Justin had said, I was unsure if it would happen. I had enjoyed success as a footballer with Cork but my under-age hurling career had not lived up to my expectations.

Also, I was still not sure that I would be in the country the following year. My employment situation was not fully resolved by then.

In the build-up to Christmas I met Denis Hurley. He was a Sarsfields man and a Cork selector. He suggested that I was in the thoughts of Justin, Fr O'Brien and the rest of the selection committee. I knew I would have Denis's support but did not expect the call-up to come so soon.

Cork had organised a number of friendly games for late January, 1985. I was already back in training with the footballers when the word came through that I had been called up to the senior hurling panel. My schedule was not getting any easier or more manageable.

On Saturday, January 27, I travelled to Cappoquin. Cork were playing

Waterford and I was informed on arrival that I would be playing. The game went by in a blur. I have only a faint recollection of it now. I must have played alright because I was selected to play in the National Hurling League the following Sunday, against Galway.

I suppose I officially became a dual player then at senior level. Certainly the extent of my commitment became very evident. I was also selected to play for the footballers on the same day, February 3, against Armagh.

I was too young, inexperienced and probably a bit overwhelmed by what was happening. To this day I don't know how it was decided that I would play with the footballers. That set the pattern for the rest of my career. Although my competitive debut would have to wait, I started training with the hurlers and was a member of the extended squad that year without forcing myself into contention for the Championship.

Off the field, my life had also taken a turn for the better when I was made permanent on the production line in Beamish & Crawford. It was the start of a love affair that would last a decade and a half. I was bringing home a wage every week and didn't have time to spend it. That I was able to give something back to my mother after all her sacrifices was a great feeling. I was on a rollercoaster that just seemed to be travelling faster and faster. I rolled with it, not thinking about the demands or the excesses.

This was my life.

The one downer, which I will go into in much more detail later, was playing my first senior football Championship game against Kerry and losing. I had been slowly introduced to the team over a period of about sixteen months and was given a starting berth at centre half-forward for the 1985 Munster final. I was moved to midfield and I played well. But we were beaten by a Kerry team that was brimming with confidence. It was a terrible experience and I vowed that, one day, I would come out on top, and sooner rather than later.

Consolation came with the Under-21 team. We were lucky to beat Tipperary that year but then coasted to the All-Ireland final where we would meet Derry, made up of most of the players who had beaten us in the minor final two years earlier. We were a different team. Paddy Hayes and Paul McGrath had emerged during the year. Tony Davis was our captain, and

Michael Slocum was playing good football. He had a great final. I scored two points and we beat them 0-14 to 1-8.

"You know, lads," Bob Honohan said to a few of us afterwards "only one team has ever won three Under-21 All-Irelands in a row. Guess who?"

Kerry, of course!

I resolved there and then to help Cork win another title, even though I had no idea about what was about to happen to my career and my life.

I was a privileged young man. I was playing hurling and football every night of the week. I was working in a good job. My first week's wage was £97. If I had been on social welfare I would have got £30. When my tax situation was sorted out and I stopped paying emergency tax, I brought home £130 every week. It was huge money at the time. I also worked overtime when I could. I wasn't able to spend the money. I would give some to my mother and keep a few pounds for a few pints, and I mean 'a few', and some other small luxuries. The rest went into my TSB account.

I remember one time checking the balance and I had about £10,000. It was incredible wealth for one who had known the other side of life. I wasn't being clever or safe with my money. I just didn't have the time or the opportunity to spend it. My priority was to give my mother whatever she would take. The rest I just put away.

At the start of 1986 I made another resolution – to have a holiday. I had always missed having a holiday when I was growing up. Our family circumstances and my involvement in sport had denied me the opportunity. Now, I had the money and I was determined to make the time.

It was a decision that would define my career and in many ways the rest of my life.

Here I am in the front (above) in a family photo which has nearly all the family: I'm with my mother and father, Mary and Denis, my Uncle Liam, his wife Nonie, Mick 'Perkins' Hayes, my baby sister, Mary, Breda, Ellen, Philly and Denis. With my mother and father on Patrick Street in Cork (right).

My mother, Mary, with Denis and me on the day of his Holy Communion; and (inset) my father, Denis, on a visit to Lourdes.

With my sisters, Philly, Mary and Ellen at Christmas.

Three generations of McCarthys, with my uncles Barry, Ted and Liam, and also my brothers, Denis and Pat (above), and (below) my sons, Niall and Cian, with their friend, Billy O'Leary – each of them in my All-Ireland winning jerseys.

*With my niece,
Helena, and John
Considine, and
Liam MacCarthy
and Sam Maguire
Cups, in 1990.*

*Our daughter,
Sinead,
celebrates her
first birthday
with the boys,
Cian and Niall.*

My mother with Niall after he won a medal at his school sports day.

Cian's a proud young man as he collects his first medal, with the winning St Joseph's Primary School team, in 2000.

Myself and Pat with Denis on his wedding day.

With Oonagh and her sister, Laura, on our wedding day and (right) Oonagh and I commence the celebrations.

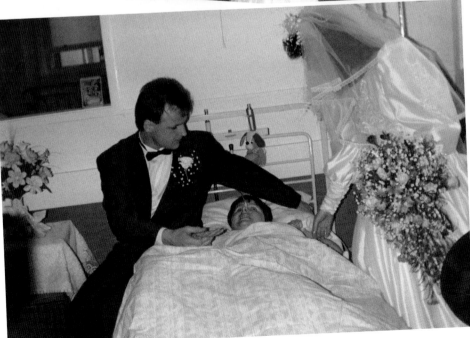

Our wedding day had so many happy memories,
Oonagh and I visit my sister, Ellen, in hospital.

Oonagh and my mother celebrate another victory in 1989 and (below) with my mother and Edward 'Nedser' Curran.

My mother and our three children, Cian, Niall and Sinead.

Oonagh and I in the year I made history, 1990, by becoming the first man to play on winning All-Ireland football and hurling teams – and Cian gets to work by trying to slip into both the Sam Maguire and Liam MacCarthy Cups.

Myself and Eddie O'Connell with the Cork senior hurling trophy, in 2008.

My mother with our great family friend, Mickey Barry, who bought me my first pair of new boots – they were Gola!

The Imokilly team which won the senior football Championship in 1984.

Teddy in action for Sarsfields, and (bottom) the Sarsfields team which lost the Cork senior final to Glen Rovers in 1989.

I walk through the streets of Thurles with Clare's Anthony Daly on the 'Torch Parade' on our way to Semple Stadium to celebrate the great old ground's 125th anniversary.

CHAPTER**6**

LIVING THE DREAM

I lived the dream in 1986.

I became the real-life comic book hero of a tale that would have been considered too fanciful if scriptwriters had offered it for publication. And I did everything I could to turn it into a nightmare.

Belligerent, stubborn, mulish, stupid. Maybe arrogant. All of those adjectives applied to me in August of that year. Instead of accepting the good fortune that was being cast in my direction with grace and gratitude, I tried to throw it all away.

To this day, I cannot understand how I got away with my behaviour in the build-up to the All-Ireland hurling final in 1986. If a player I coached behaved with me the way I behaved with Johnny Clifford and other legendary figures in Cork hurling, I would banish him forever.

In short, I was being offered a chance to make my Championship debut for the Cork senior hurling team in the All-Ireland final and I was insisting on taking a holiday in the Canary Islands, refusing point blank to change my plans.

I was insane and, worse still, I knew it.

I was out of control but not in the way those intimately involved with the situation imagined. I knew that I was wrong but I could not bring myself to take the steps that would make everything all right. Now, 26 years later, I still cannot explain it.

Outwardly, it might have looked like I was sure of myself at the time but, inside, I was choking with emotion. Instead of feeling elated at the prospect of being involved in an All-Ireland final, I was battling with a sense of dread and doom and, still, I persisted with my act of madness.

It is possible that I was overwhelmed by the speed with which I moved into the picture. It wasn't until August of that year that I first got an inkling I was featuring in the thoughts of the team management and, even then, I found it hard to take in. It all seemed unreal.

I had not reached my 20th birthday when I was first called in to train with the Cork senior hurlers, during the winter months of 1984 and '85. I was now involved with ten different teams but this latest addition, I felt, was the least taxing. I felt I was just making up the numbers in training and wasn't included in match day squads. I did play a few challenge games and was selected for the National Hurling League but could not play because of a clash with a football game.

It suited me not to be too closely involved with the senior hurlers as competition began in 1986, because I was so busy elsewhere. I had played for the Munster footballers that year in the old Railway Cup competition, alongside the Spillane brothers, Tom and Mick, Jack O'Shea and Tommy Doyle, as far as I can remember. I enjoyed the experience though I would have been better off without further demands on my time.

I certainly enjoyed training with the senior hurlers. I knew lads like Tony O'Sullivan and Tomas Mulcahy from school. I had played Under-21 hurling for Cork with Jim Cashman and we had become friends. There were familiar faces from various football teams I played with, like Denis Walsh, Kevin Hennessy and Denis Mulcahy.

There were other players there that I had admired from a distance – John Crowley, Tom Cashman, Dermot McCurtain, Pat Hartnett, John Fenton and the great Jimmy Barry Murphy. They were multiple All-Ireland winners, household names throughout Ireland.

Johnny Clifford was the coach. A mild-mannered, nice man, he was one of the most respected figures in hurling in the city and county, and was an All-Ireland medal winner himself. So, too, was one of his selectors, Jimmy Brohan. Another selector was my old teacher, Donal O'Grady who had retired from playing after winning an All-Ireland title in 1984.

I was neither overawed nor over-excited. It became part of my routine. My expectations were not all that high. I was concentrating mainly on the club and the county Under-21 footballers and hurlers.

Although hurling was my first love I wasn't having much success with Cork. The Under-21s again made an early exit from the Championship when we were beaten by Clare in the Munster semi-final. We retained our Under-21 provincial football title beating Kerry and Tipperary, the latter only marginally.

I played for the senior football team in the Munster final against Kerry. They didn't play well. Even Mikey Sheehy had a bad day with his free-taking. And still we lost! I was getting fed up with the sight of that Kerry jersey already.

Two weeks later, on July 21, Cork played Clare in the Munster hurling final in Killarney. I was one of the six subs named on the Tuesday evening before the game. The team was largely made up of the players who had won the All-Ireland in 1984, with the addition of Denis Walsh, Jim Cashman at wing-forward and John Fitzgibbon at right corner-forward.

Clare had a mixed bag of a team. There were veterans like Ger Loughnane, Sean Stack and Johnny Callinan mixed in with young lads like Tommy Guilfoyle, but it proved to be a much tighter game than people expected. Guilfoyle scored two goals and two points. John Fitzgibbon got a crucial goal for us, and we won by 2-18 to 3-12.

The selectors made just one change during the game. It didn't involve me. I sat on the bench not really feeling a part of the whole thing. I didn't believe that the selectors really gave me any consideration – I might as well have been sitting in the stands for all I was contributing.

Once again the Under-21 football team was my focus. We were due to play Derry in the All-Ireland semi-final in Parnell Park, on August 10, a Saturday evening. Cork would play Antrim in the All-Ireland senior hurling semi-final the following day in Croke Park. The second semi-final between Galway and Kilkenny would be played in Thurles. My priority was the football game. We had built up a great rivalry with this bunch of Derry players over the previous two seasons at minor and Under-21 level and there was a lot of respect between us. I didn't give the hurling game a thought.

No one in Cork did. No one gave Antrim a chance. After my experience in the Munster final I decided to focus all my energy on the football game.

It was another close, tight contest. We won it by two points, 1-13 to 2-8, and there was a great sense of achievement afterwards, and I was mingling with some of the other players and officials when I met Johnny Clifford. He congratulated me on the win and then asked me to step aside for a chat.

He told me quietly that he understood I would be tired and that I wouldn't expect to be involved the following day but he wanted to be sure that I was there with the rest of the hurling panel. "I want you there with us, to be part of the game," he said, or words to that effect. I didn't realise – nor didn't want to know – that it was his way of telling me to stick with them and my chance could come.

"Of course, Johnny, no bother," I replied.

In my mind I had no intention of being there. I had just won an All-Ireland semi-final and that was enough for me for one weekend. Why would I waste a Sunday in Dublin sitting in a stand watching a game that Cork were certain to win? I wanted to get back to Cork.

We were staying at The Burlington Hotel, as usual, and the hurlers were billeted there as well. I slept well that night and rose early. After a quick breakfast I made my way to Heuston Station to get the train back to Cork, leaving my colleagues behind me. The train was already rolling as I walked through the carriages looking for a quiet place to sit. It was then I encountered Bob Honohan and Jerry Lucey, who was an Under-21 selector with Bob.

"Where are you going, you're supposed to be with the hurlers?" was the reaction. "You'll have to get off at the first stop and take the next train back."

"No way, lads," I said. "I'm getting back to Cork as quick as I can."

Little did they or anyone back in The Burlington Hotel know that I had one other surprise in store.

•••••

I had celebrated my 21st birthday on July 1, 1986, and that's when I realised that, apart from a night away in some place like Youghal, I had never been on a proper holiday.

Most of the people I knew had, at one time or another, taken time to fly to sunny destinations in the Mediterranean or other exotic places that the tour operators advertised heavily in the 1970s and '80s. I was simply too busy working, and playing hurling and football, to have the time for such a luxury.

During that summer I decided it was time I got the opportunity to spend some of the money in my bank account and to enjoy some of the simple pleasures of life. I was doing a line with Liz Dunphy at the time. We chatted about having a holiday and I mentioned that I would love to go to the Canary Islands.

Liz played camogie for Sarsfields and Cork, and she was as aware as anyone of my commitments. We talked about dates and I told her not to worry about me. I knew the dates for the Under-21 games and that was all I was thinking about. I wasn't getting my game with the senior hurlers and, up to then, I had no indication that that was about to change. We booked a two-week package to start on August 14.

As usual on the Tuesday night after the All-Ireland semi-final, I attended a training session in Pairc Ui Chaoimh. Johnny took me to one side before the session and expressed his disappointment in me. It was unheard of in Cork that a player would be asked to attend a Championship game as part of the panel and not turn up. Johnny could not understand how a young player would behave that way.

I didn't say very much to him.

I still couldn't see the point of sitting on the bench for the afternoon. He sensed I wasn't paying a lot of heed to what he was saying.

"Teddy, you have to give a commitment now," he began. "You have to show people that you are serious about all of this."

I gave him an assurance. I told him that I was committed to Cork and wanted to play for the county and would work hard in training to prove myself. He seemed relieved and the conversation was reaching its conclusion.

"There's just one thing, Johnny," I said.

"I'm going on holidays on Saturday."

"What!" he almost shouted. "What do you mean?"

When I explained my plans and that I had already paid for the holiday he immediately told me he would get the money and reimburse me. I was to cancel the holiday. I was not to go.

I refused.

It should have been obvious to me then that the management were taking a closer interest in me. Johnny didn't say it straight out that I might be involved in the final but his interest should have been enough. Over the next few days the obvious began to dawn on me. I didn't know what to do and didn't know where to turn or who to talk to.

A number of people rang me and advised me not to go on holiday. Don Hegarty, the Human Resources Manager at Beamish & Crawford, spoke to me. In any other circumstance, if Don had told me to jump I would have asked how high. He brought me into the company because I was a GAA man, not because I had impressed him in an interview.

Don asked me about the situation and gently suggested that this time I should postpone my holiday, make the sacrifice for Cork hurling. If he had threatened to sack me I probably would have cancelled the holiday. He would never have done anything like that and gentle persuasion wasn't going to work.

On the Thursday night in Pairc Ui Chaoimh, I was almost sick with worry. I think by then I knew I was making a mistake but I remained reluctant to give in. Was I just being stubborn? I suppose so.

Donal O'Grady met me in the tunnel. He tried to persuade me. He was very nice about it and just told me that I was taking a chance with my career and that there could be consequences down the line. I could go on holidays every year but I might not get another chance of playing in an All-Ireland final with Cork.

I was wavering.

But Donal didn't know that. The evidence before him was a young lad telling him over and over that he was going on holiday anyway, no matter what anyone said. Eventually he walked away.

He could not have known that I was on the verge of changing my mind. Another couple of minutes and I would have relented. Instead, I walked out to my car. Once I closed the door I began to cry. What am I after doing? I asked myself. I thought I had just made the biggest mistake of my life.

I was sick with worry and confusion for the next twenty-four hours. No one knew what was going on inside me. I was always good at hiding my emotions. By the time we flew out on Saturday morning I was getting into holiday mood. I had two weeks of sunshine to look forward to. I was going on a new adventure, and within a few days I had forgotten about the turmoil of the days before departure. The beach, the beer and the sunshine helped me unwind. For the first time in a few years I forgot about hurling and football.

I certainly had no idea what the Cork hurling management were thinking. If I had been asked while relaxing by the pool I would have guessed they weren't thinking about me any more.

●●●●●

We got back to Glanmire on Saturday, August 28. There were a few items of correspondence waiting for me. One was a letter from GAA Headquarters in Croke Park. I had been invited to attend a trial at Croke Park the following day for the Compromise Rules team that would travel to Australia later in the year. It was a nice surprise. The team was being coached by the legendary Kevin Heffernan, and it was an attraction in itself to have the opportunity to meet the man.

A few phone calls later and I found out a few of the other lads were also going up for the trial – Jimmy Kerrigan, Niall Cahalane and John O'Driscoll had been asked along as well. At least the train journey the following morning would be a bit of craic. None of the envelopes carried the Cork GAA crest. There hadn't been any phone calls from Pairc Ui Chaoimh.

Later in the evening I rambled down to the GAA pitch. Glanmire were playing Mayfield in a League match. It was a fierce local rivalry with only pride at stake. After two weeks enjoying myself I thought it would be great to play again. I went home and got my gear, and it was when I arrived back at the pitch that I first got an inkling of what was on the rumour mill.

Timmy Walsh was a selector with Glanmire. He had been involved with Cork teams and knew many of the people with the county board. In conversations, while I was away, he had been told that the Cork selectors were still considering me for a place in the team for the All-Ireland final. He didn't tell me that but tried to dissuade me from playing. "You're on the panel for the final, you shouldn't chance playing here," he told me.

I insisted on playing.

I got support from Tim Nyhan. He was a great Glanmire man, a great character and a father figure in the club. We were playing Mayfield and he wanted to win that game more than he wanted Cork to win the All-Ireland. There was murder on the sideline as the selectors argued over whether I would play or not.

Tim got his way.

I started.

That's when the murder spread to the pitch.

As I said, there was nothing at stake but pride. And there is nothing more sure to cause trouble on a pitch than pride. There were very few people at the game but they were almost coming in over the fence to get at us. On the field there were belts flying. Whatever rustiness was in my limbs was quickly shaken out of them.

The referee was a man named Ned Porter. He was from the Brian Dillons club on the north side of the city and was a great guy. He had more to worry about than me but he did worry. Ned was aware of the speculation about me playing in the All-Ireland. In fact, he had better information than most.

At one stage during one of the many breaks in the game, he went over to our selectors. "Listen lads, it's almost certain that Teddy will be playing on Sunday week. I don't want to have to send him off … so will you please take him off?"

I responded. "I couldn't be on the team after what I've done. That's mad. I'm playing on." Minutes later I was soloing up the line with the ball. I sensed someone coming on my left; I sneaked a glance over my right shoulder and saw another fella coming from there. I was to be the meat in a sandwich. I didn't even have time to pass the ball. The guy on my right was closest.

I swung back with my elbow, and caught him on the chin.

As a fierce row broke out, I felt a strong arm on my elbow and heard Timmy Walsh say, "Let's get out of here." He almost carried me across the width of the pitch and threw me into his car.

"What about my gear?" I roared.

His response was unpleasant but understandable in the circumstances. As Ned Porter abandoned the game I was already at home cleaning up. I travelled to Dublin on Sunday morning with the other Cork players. Kerrigan was in his usual form, slagging me mercilessly. But there was no talk of the hurling final. I think we were all dreaming about the chance of getting a month in Australia.

Late on Sunday night the telephone rang at home.

It was Johnny Clifford.

He was as nice as ever and asked me to assure him I would be at training on Tuesday night. I promised I would and told him I was in good shape. I'd had a few drinks on holiday and ate well but I had not overdone it. I was as fit as a flea anyway and had felt good in Dublin that day when Heffo and Liam Sammon from Galway had put us through a demanding enough session. But I still didn't expect to play in the final.

There was no attention on me on Tuesday evening. Richard Brown was working as a dentist in Kent at the time and all the talk was about him being able to return for the game. When it came to the announcement of the team, I was just about paying attention.

Ger Cunningham, Denis Mulcahy, Richard Brown, John Crowley, Pat Hartnett, Tom Cashman the team captain…

As expected.

I was daydreaming by now.

Then I heard the name Denis Walsh.

Delighted for him, I thought.

No.8, John Fenton… No.9 Jim Cashman. Again I looked up. A big smile lit up underneath his red curls.

No.10, Teddy McCarthy.

"What the … it can't be! Jesus Christ almighty."

I looked around.

The lads were looking straight ahead at Johnny. I didn't hear the rest of the team. Tomas Mulcahy, Tony O'Sullivan, Ger Fitzgerald, Jimmy Barry Murphy, Kevin Hennessy. The subs were named – Frank O'Sullivan, John O'Callaghan, Cathal Casey, John Meyler, Kieran Kingston and John Fitzgibbon. It was all a blur to me. I only came to my senses when a couple of players gave me a pat on the back.

I drove home in a daze.

Only my mother and Mary were there. I told them I was on the team. They didn't create a fuss, just said well done. Naturally, it caused a bit of a fuss in the newspapers the following day. The lads at work knocked great fun from the description of me as a "dual star rebel" in one newspaper.

The days flew by. We talked about Galway in a couple of meetings. They had a very good half-back line of Pete Finnerty, Tony Keady and Gerry McInerney. They had been match winners in the shock semi-final win over Kilkenny. I would be marked by McInerney. Ger Cunningham would be sending some puck outs in my direction. I was to disrupt the influence of that line with my fielding and by running at them.

Everyone I met that week talked hurling and the final. I was almost oblivious to the excitement and to the attention. I felt no pressure. I was calm, almost too laid back. That would be shaken out of me before the game started.

We travelled to Dublin by train on the Saturday. I was rooming with Jim Cashman. That was good. We had played Minor football and hurling together and had become friends. We were relaxed in each other's company. There was no danger we would be overcome by nerves anyway.

After breakfast on Sunday morning we had some time to kill. We were sitting in our room looking for something to do when Jim said: "Come on, we'll head down to Jimmy Barry Murphy's room."

Jimmy was rooming with John Crowley.

They'd had the Sunday newspapers delivered to the room. These old hands had the routine well sorted. Between them they had won multiple All-Ireland medals. They were coming to the end of their careers but were still hugely influential. John had broken a thumb in the early rounds of the Championship and had worked very hard to get fit for the latter stages.

I picked up the *Sunday Independent* and began to read. The emphasis seemed to be on Galway. Their players were eulogised, especially the half-backs. I was interrupted. It was Jimmy.

"Well, Teddy, do you think we'll do it today?"

Here was the great Jimmy Barry Murphy, one of the icons of hurling, not just in Cork but all over Ireland, talking to a kid from Glanmire in his hotel room on the morning of an All-Ireland final. It was all a bit hard to take in. I didn't really know what to say to him. I was a little overwhelmed by the whole scenario.

I gave him a glib answer.

Waving the newspaper at him, I said: "According to this we'll be really up against it Jimmy, don't think so... No."

Johnny Crowley sprang across the room.

He jabbed me in the chest.

"What did you say?

"What was that?" he shouted.

I tried to say that I was just repeating what the papers were saying. I was trying to be intelligent. The papers are never wrong, are they?

"You'd want to change your attitude," said Johnny. "If you don't, you might not be playing at all."

Here was a man who had toiled for ten years or more for Cork. He had given everything, taken all the hard knocks, broken bones, traipsed all over Ireland and made every sacrifice possible. This was likely to be his last final. And here was this kid helicoptered into a final, as if I was invented for the day, a whippersnapper with an attitude playing his first senior game and saying he didn't think Cork would win.

As Johnny, again, thrust his fist into my chest Jim, who was sitting quietly in the corner, burst out laughing.

"What's so funny?" Johnny roared at him.

It was 11am and it was only then I fully realised what was at stake, what the game was worth and what it meant. Up to then, it was just another game for me. Because of the way I had prepared I was absolutely calm coming up to the final. I had no nerves at all. That helped me in one way. I didn't have sleepless nights and I didn't waste any energy worrying.

But I did need something to lift me, something to spark the competitive fires in my inexperienced mind. I learned a lot from Johnny Crowley that morning. It served me well for the rest of my career.

By the time we were leaving the hotel for the game I was in a better frame of mind. I still enjoyed the atmosphere. Cork supporters jammed the hotel.

It was harder to get out of there than it was to play in the final. Our minors had also qualified for the final where they would play Offaly. David Walsh from Sarsfields had played earlier in the Championship and was a substitute for the final. I watched some of that game and David came on in the forward line. They lost to a really good Offaly team that would provide players to win a number of senior titles in the years to come.

I enjoyed our final.

It was a tactical game. Galway had played a two-man full-forward line in the semi-final against Kilkenny, bringing the third man, nominally the right corner-forward, out around the middle of the field. Kilkenny weren't prepared for it and Joe Cooney had gleefully exploited the space. Johnny Clifford decided that if they did it again Johnny Crowley was to stay in his orthodox position and not to follow the roving player. It worked a treat. Galway fired ball after ball in to Johnny and he dealt with it brilliantly.

It was a high-scoring, all-action final.

We won by 4-13 to 2-15. I was the only Cork forward not to score.

Kieran Kingston, who came on for John Fenton, even scored a couple of points. But I made my contribution. I played a lot of ball and created lots of chances. I had been selected to subdue the Galway half-back line and I did that. John Fenton scored a goal from a free early on. Kevin Hennessy scored the first of two goals in the first half. Tomas Mul got a great individual goal at the start of the second half, and Kevin's second, and our fourth, goal was the clincher.

I got an insight into what made guys like Barry Murphy, Crowley, Fenton and Tom Cashman so successful. They never rested. The game was almost over when I got a ball about sixty yards from their goal, on the Cusack Stand side of the pitch. Jimmy made a run and I should have given him a pass. But I went for my score and put it wide. He didn't rant or rave, just told me that I had taken the wrong option. The game was won but he would not stop seeking perfection until the final whistle was blown.

There was a lot of emotion at the end. It was Jimmy's last game for Cork. We knew there were others who would not return, men who had given great service to Cork for many years. I began to realise the enormity of what had happened as we assembled on the steps of the Hogan Stand. It was my first time experiencing the delirium of the supporters as they mobbed us on the field. The smile on Tom Cashman's face as he lifted the Liam McCarthy Cup lit up Croke Park.

Despite the celebrations in both Croke Park and back at the hotel, the enormity of the occasion did not strike me until I got home the following day. I enjoyed the Sunday night, but it was when I saw the crowds at the station in Cork and all along the route to Patrick Street that I first understood what something like this meant to the people of Cork.

What also struck me was the pleasure in the faces of the experienced players. Jimmy Barry Murphy had won his fifth All-Ireland hurling medal and his sixth in all, when you add in the football medal he won in 1973. Yet he was as happy now as I was with my first success. I would never have believed it before that night but the homecoming was actually better than winning the game itself. I know that will sound strange but you have to experience it to understand it.

On a personal level, there was one other special night. I was allowed to bring the Liam McCarthy Cup back to Glanmire. We didn't have a clubhouse at the time so a reception was arranged in the Castle Tavern by the then owners, Angela and Mick Murphy.

That was a big night for my mother and the rest of the family. I knew they were proud of what I had achieved, even though it wasn't said. But that night was as much for them and the people of Glanmire as it was for me. My mother was the centre of attention. She was more important than I was and she was totally taken aback. She was the Queen of the town for a few hours and she deserved it. I had a God-given talent and I was lucky to be playing with great players and being coached by great coaches. The real truth was what people were saying to her.

"You did a great job, Mary."

On that evening, all the scrubbing and cleaning, all the minding and protecting, all the worrying had been rewarded.

While everyone was celebrating for days, I was back in training. The Under-21 footballers played Offaly in the All-Ireland final the following Sunday. Michael McCarthy and Paul McGrath tormented our opposition. Paul scored 1-7, Mick kicked 0-6. We won by 3-16 to 0-12. Three-in-a-row. We had matched Kerry's achievement in the grade and the sense of satisfaction was enormous. It was the seed for success in the years ahead.

I was having an incredible time. Just a few weeks later I got the news that I had been selected to travel with the Ireland Compromise Rules team to compete against the professionals of the Australian Football League in the Southern Hemisphere. We would be away from home for four weeks on what promised to be the trip of a lifetime.

That it certainly was.

•••••

It was about nine o'clock on the night of October 18. We were packed into the bar of the team hotel in Adelaide, the capital of the state of Victoria. The Ireland team was celebrating a victory in the Second Test against Australia to tie the series, joined by supporters and the small group of journalists who had travelled with the squad.

We were already two weeks into the tour and the squad of players from the four corners of Ireland had formed a close bond. It was a unified bunch. You mixed with everyone, not just the lads from your own county.

The booze was flowing freely.

We knew nothing about Australian beer. Fosters was even new to us. VB wasn't a great taste. A lot of us were drinking vodka and orange. Screwdrivers. I wasn't getting much of a buzz from them. Joe McNally, the big Dublin forward and sound character, took me by the elbow.

"Get over here and try this," said Joe. "It's yer only man."

Southern Comfort.

It was perfect.

I was nicely settled when Kevin Heffernan walked in. Our manager had given us permission to celebrate and was joining us for a few minutes. He chatted with Mick Holden and Niall Cahalane for a while. They had struck up a great friendship on the tour. You could easily see that Heffernan and Holden were close. Holden had a great sense of humour and was the perfect foil to Heffernan's more serious approach to life. Then Heffernan came over to where myself and McNally were standing.

"Well, Teddy, what did you think of that?" he asked.

"Jesus, Kevin, it was super," I replied.

"We've given ourselves a great chance of winning the series. What if I asked you to play next Friday night, what would you do for me?" Heffernan asked. I was caught a bit off-guard. I had played in a warm up game in a place called Bunbury, in Western Australia, on the first week of the tour but was only used as the water carrier in the First Test in Perth, which we lost.

In the week between the First and Second Tests I was one of the players allowed to go to the many receptions which were laid on for the tourists. We drank all the wine and ate all the cheese we could get, knowing that if the boss was releasing us for these events we would not be playing in Melbourne.

Now, Kevin was bringing up the possibility of me playing in the deciding Test. I gave him some silly answer like, "I'll do my best." Heffernan didn't accept an answer like that.

"I want to see you in my room at midnight," he said. "See if you can come up with a better reply."

He was friendly about it but I knew that was one appointment I could not miss. That was the end of the Southern Comfort for that night. McNally was laughing at me. I went over to Gerry Hargan and asked him what I should say to Heffernan later. For some reason he laughed as well.

Surely Mick Holden could help? He knew the man better than anyone.

"Tell him you'll stop drinking for the night," was his helpful contribution.

It was like going for an interview. I was outside his door five minutes before midnight. At twelve o'clock I knocked on the door. He told me to come in. He was lying on the bed and had a glass of red wine on the locker.

I sat on a chair at the end of the bed.

We exchanged some small-talk and then he asked, "Did you think about it?" I said I had, but I repeated almost exactly what I had said earlier.

"Teddy," he said, "I could go down now to the front door of the hotel and stop the first man passing by and ask him what he would do to play for Ireland and he would say the same thing to me. Go away now and think about it and we'll talk again tomorrow."

I was awake all night.

I hoped that Liam Sammon would take the training session the next day so that I wouldn't have to meet Heffernan. As we gathered at the team bus to go to training I was hiding behind the lads. The closer we got to the door of the bus the better I felt. There was no sign of him. I was beginning to breathe a sigh of relief when he appeared at my shoulder.

"What's your answer?"

"Fucking hell, Kevin, all I can say is that I will run till I drop."

"That's what I wanted to hear," he replied.

Kevin Heffernan had a huge impact on all of us who went to Australia. We were in awe of him. He never raised his voice. In the dressing room and at team meetings his voice kept to the same pitch at all times. He was always in control of himself and every situation. But he would get the adrenaline pumping in you with his motivational talks. He was amazing, so intelligent.

Sitting beside him at games, it was incredible how easily he could read the game and make changes that made such a difference. He was very intelligent, so focussed and insightful. He brought a fairly mixed group of footballers and personalities, and made us a very unified group and team.

I met guys like Pat O'Byrne from Wicklow, a horse of a man. Brian McGilligan from Derry was another powerful, physical man. I became great friends with Willie Doyle from Carlow and Ciaran Murray from Monaghan. I love to see Ciaran working with the Republic of Ireland soccer team these days as a physiotherapist. He was a schoolteacher then but went back to college to retrain.

Heffernan was meticulous in his planning. I remember before we went on tour he gave Jimmy Kerrigan, Niall Cahalane, John O'Driscoll and myself a lift to Heuston Station. He discovered we had paid our own train fares. He was furious. We were reimbursed and we didn't have to pay again.

I'm not sure I fulfilled his expectations in the Third Test in Adelaide. It was a horrible night. There was a storm raging, with high winds and heavy rain. I started the match and got involved with one of the Australians. There was a fair bit of trash talk going on. Then a couple of punches were thrown.

It was happening all over the field. They had decided from the start of the Series that they were going to intimidate us physically. They didn't like it when we hit back.

After the Second Test their coach, a fiery little lad called John Todd, described us as "wimps" and criticised our reaction to their physical play. I think they were a bit cocky, that they didn't rate us, and were unsure how to play us.

Anyway, myself and the Australian both got warnings. The Australians were cute. They immediately switched another player onto me. He started giving me lip and then the physical stuff began. I let him at it for a while but, eventually, I snapped.

I lashed out.

He got a card, I got a second and was ordered to the line. As I was walking off, one of their interchange players started shouting abuse at me. My game was over and this clown was not going to get away with it. I went for him. The problem was that one of the sideline TV cameras was in my way. I was trying to get at him, screaming abuse and he was screaming back, and the camera was following me all the way. The lads back home watching the game on television were loving it.

We won that Third Test. John O'Driscoll was sensational. I was delighted for him. It brought a memorable trip to a brilliant end. We had started out in Perth in the first week of October. We moved to Melbourne, a lovely city where we had great fun. Adelaide was next, and then we spent a few days in Sydney for relaxation. It is an experience that I will never forget.

My extraordinary year concluded with Imokilly regaining the Cork senior football title, and doing so dramatically. St Finbarr's were again the opposition and their team was packed with talented footballers – John Kerins, John Meyler, Mick Slocum, Paddy Hayes, Tony Leahy, Christy Ryan, Kieran McCarthy and Dave Barry were just some of those who played against us.

Hayes and myself had a great battle in the middle of the field. Conor Counihan was also playing well at centre half-back for us. It was just as well because the 'Barrs were giving us a pounding for a long time and should have been comfortably in front. In fact, they must wonder to this day how they lost the game because we didn't even manage to score in the first half. That in itself is hard to believe but, even all these years later, it is harder to understand how we managed to turn it around.

Brian Lotty can boast that he certainly made a difference. He came on as a sub in the second half and was fouled for a penalty, which Robert Swaine converted to give us a glimmer of hope. They led by two points in the last minute when Tadhg Murphy won the ball and handpassed it to Brian who scored a winning goal.

We were champions, 2-4 to 0-9.

What a year.

CHAPTER 7

GREEN AND GOLD

Kerry.

Just five letters, yet the word those letters form inflames emotions in me like no other.

I have the greatest respect for Kerry football and its traditions. And I was, like tens of thousands of others, a great admirer of the football team that graced the fields of Munster and Ireland in the 1970s and half of the 1980s.

At the same time, I was obsessed with the desire to beat them. Nothing, and I stress nothing, gave me more pleasure in my football career than playing against and beating Kerry.

Winning a Munster final against Kerry in Pairc Ui Chaoimh or Fitzgerald Stadium in Killarney was better than winning the All-Ireland Championship. Once we had Kerry beaten, my ambitions for the year were satisfied. I know that sounds insane but it is the truth. I played my best football against Kerry in the Munster Championship.

With the possible exception of the 1989 All-Ireland final, I don't think I ever carried my Munster football form into Croke Park. My two favourite football grounds were Pairc Ui Chaoimh, which we know here in Cork as The Park, and Killarney. When hurling, I loved Thurles. Croke Park never appealed to me. It was always great to get to Croke Park because of the unique place it is for all GAA people and because of the significance of each occasion, but I never liked the surface. It was like walking through a field with all its dips and hollows.

Just by virtue of being born in Cork you grow up with an attitude about Kerry. Some might call it a complex. Well, that annoyed me, too. I was aware from an early age that Kerry football people felt they had a God-given right to beat Cork every year. The fact that it seemed to happen with great regularity made me even madder.

I was just a kid when Mick O'Dwyer became their manager, in 1974, and began to build a new team that would dominate Gaelic football for the best part of twelve years. At the same time, in Cork, we had our own super team – the hurlers – who won three All-Ireland senior Championships in a row between 1976 and 1978. We also had our football heroes, the players who won the All-Ireland title in 1973. But we seemed to live in the shadow of the Kerry team, subservient, manacled to their greatness.

That 1973 Cork football team would almost certainly have achieved a lot more if Kerry and Micko had not come along. I wasn't a great reader growing up, but Pat Fahy, with whom I worked on Saturdays, loved to read the newspapers and voraciously fed on coverage of hurling and football, especially Munster finals. Back then, the *Cork Examiner* seemed to publish special editions every year for the Munster finals involving Cork. I remember being in Pat's van and picking up the *Examiner* the day before Cork would play Kerry. Every year it was the same old mantra.

Mick O'Dwyer: "Cork are the second-best team in Ireland, we always find them the hardest team to beat."

The players would all speak similarly.

"Cork are so tough." Or: "With the talent they have we know we're going to have a hard game." On and on it went. The same old platitudes worded just a little differently.

Year after year we were patronised. And they would go out on Sunday and beat Cork by ten or twelve points. They never beat anyone else by that much or that easily, it seemed to me. But when it came to early July the next year they would say exactly the same crap. Even as a teenager it drove me crazy. I felt they were laughing at us and I couldn't bear it. Reading those supplements I would be seething and I dreamed of the day when I would be able to do something about it.

I always loved going to Killarney.

My very first time going there with the senior footballers was in 1984. It was my 19th birthday and I was filled with excitement getting onto the bus at the old Jury's Hotel. I wasn't part of the squad of 21 who would tog out that day, but was being brought along for the experience. We always had a Garda escort all the way from Cork. They would close off towns like Macroom and Ballyvourney so that we could have an uninterrupted journey. Then you reached Killarney and the streets would be crowded with supporters. The sun always seemed to be shining.

I learned something important that day in 1984 that I brought with me to every future outing against Kerry. By coincidence, the two team buses arrived in Fitzgerald Stadium at the same time. For some reason there was a delay in opening the gate to the dressing room area so the players were left mingling around the entrance. I looked around me. Jack O'Shea, Pat Spillane, Mikey Sheehy, Eoin Liston, Paidi O Se, Ogie Moran, Ger Power. They were all there. The superstars of Gaelic football.

Our lads, the older players, looked at them in awe. It was all "Howya, Jacko," … "How's it going, Paidi?" … "Good man, Bomber."

All that sort of shite.

Looking up to them.

Beaten before the bloody gate had even opened.

We're going to get a hammering, I thought to myself. I felt like screaming. I wasn't even playing but my inclination was to turn my back on them.

It wasn't that I disliked them personally. At that stage I didn't know any of them. I admired them for their skill and what they had achieved. But they were the enemy for the day and I wouldn't bend the knee to them. I would be delighted to meet them and chat later when we had them beaten.

We didn't beat them that day.

They won 3-14 to 2-10.

Colman Corrigan played in midfield for us. Tadhg Murphy from Glanmire was at left corner-forward. He had scored the winning goal in the last minute of the 1983 Munster final for Cork's first win over the old enemy since 1974. There was no late drama in this game. Spillane scored two goals. They won comfortably.

The old order had been restored.

Barry Coffey was on the bench. He came on and scored a goal. I watched from the sideline, happy for Barry, but frustrated that I would have to wait at least another year for a chance to pit myself against these men. Barry and I had no fear of Kerry. We played on Cork under-age teams that didn't lose to Kerry. There were a lot of young guys about to come through who felt that way – Niall Cahalane, Tony Davis, Colm O'Neill, John Cleary and John O'Driscoll, for example. But the older players were almost conditioned to losing to Kerry.

A year later, we were coached by Denis Coughlan and there was a huge emphasis on fitness in training. With my commitments to so many teams, fitness was never an issue. I was slowly establishing myself on the senior football team and when the team for the Munster final on July 21, 1985 was named, I was in at centre half-forward. It was my first Munster final and I was playing in Pairc Ui Chaoimh.

Paddy Harrington from Doneraile was on my right, Tony Nation on my left. The full-forward line was Tony O'Sullivan (my old hurling colleague from the Mon), Colm O'Neill and Dave Barry. Barry Coffey and Martin McCarthy from Youghal were selected at midfield. At an early stage of the game I was moved to midfield. I felt good. I was moving well and fielding well. I also kicked a point. But we were still not in a position, mentally at least, to beat Kerry. They won by 2-11 to 0-11.

It didn't get any better in 1986 when Kerry beat us without ever hitting full stride. I still had the Under-21 Championship to satisfy my desire for success but I must admit I was getting fairly fed up of the sight of green and gold clad footballers dancing rings around us, and no one able to lay a hand on them.

There was no time for me to brood about losing another big game to Kerry. This eventful summer of '86 had plenty of distractions to occupy me. I was in Australia chatting to the other Cork lads one night when Jimmy Kerrigan started talking about Billy Morgan. His name was being linked to a coaching role with the Cork team and Niall, John and I wanted to know more about him. We all knew what he had done for Cork as a player and he had gained a huge reputation at Nemo Rangers as a coach. Jimmy promised us that if Billy got the Cork football job our lives would be transformed.

We were delighted to hear his enthusiasm but had no idea just how great the transformation would be. Two other men were also about to enter our lives and would considerably contribute to that change. Larry Tompkins and Shea Fahy were about to be bestowed with the honour of becoming members of the Cork citizenry.

•••••

Billy Morgan is Mr Football in Cork.

He is to the big ball game what Jimmy Barry Murphy is to hurling. He is an icon. Billy doesn't just resonate with players. He is the people's champion as well. What he did for football in Cork, for his club Nemo Rangers and for the county, is beyond comprehension. He was brilliant for Cork and for me.

The first night he was introduced to us as our new coach you could sense a difference around the squad. A lot of us had come from the Under-21 set-up which was brilliantly run. But this was another level. I had seen in Australia what it was like to be involved with a professional set-up, even if it only lasted four weeks. Billy now brought professional structures and timing to our squad.

I knew him a little before then, and was well aware of his status in Cork football having been the last man from the county to lift the Sam Maguire Cup. Getting to know him better, the first thing that strikes you is his passion. I don't know if I have ever met anyone with as much passion for anything as Billy possessed for Cork football. He also shared my obsession with Kerry. It was that passion and desire that drove him, and it rubbed off on the rest of us.

He wasn't just about passion. He was very organised and had a great football brain. He was also very easy to go to if you had a problem. He would talk through those problems and help out in whatever way he could. Mary, his wife, is a real lady and she was always willing to listen if we had anything bothering us and would be a fantastic support to all of us over the next seven or eight years.

Billy knew from the start that there was a lot of talent available to him.

The Under-21 successes of the previous three seasons had provided a fresh intake of talent to supplement what was already there. But someone needed to bring all that talent and fuse it together. Billy was that man. He knew how to get the best out of individuals for the good of the team.

He also had a short fuse.

If training was not going the way he wanted and you were considered part of the problem, then you had reason to be worried. No one ever wanted to be called in for a chat when his mood was dark. He would terrify you. But the one thing we always knew was that Billy wanted the best for you as a player – what was best for Cork as well – and it was the only way we were going to start beating Kerry, and then think about winning All-Irelands.

With his temper and my habit of doing things my way it was inevitable that there would be flashpoints between us. Surprisingly they were few, although they were memorable.

I believe that with the group of players that he had available to him Billy would have guided us to an All-Ireland Championship. But the acquisition of Larry Tompkins and Shea Fahy guaranteed that we would be successful. Both of them had been very good players for their native Kildare. Shea had moved to Cork as an Army Officer and had joined Nemo where he first impressed Billy. Larry already had a big reputation from his days with Kildare. He had been spending a lot of time in America and had fallen out with the authorities in his native county. During the summers, Larry had been working in West Cork and joined Castlehaven where the football crazy people in that part of the world got an indication of what it was that had made everyone who had ever seen him play become so animated and enthralled.

Their transfers were probably a bit controversial because it was so unusual for players to switch counties. We were all fairly unconcerned about it. At the time, I remember wondering if we really needed two guys from outside when we had so much talent in Cork. It was obvious that they were two very good footballers and I was happy enough to welcome them, if it meant we had a better chance of finally beating Kerry in a Munster final.

Shea was an out-and-out midfielder. Danny Culloty, Barry Coffey, Larry and myself could play there as well but we could also be switched to the half-forward line and even the half-back line if needed. I think Larry could have played anywhere. He had so much natural ability but he also worked so hard. It almost frightened me to hear the sort of training he was doing. We heard about daily cycles from Cork to Mitchelstown and back on the old Dublin road, up and down those hills, punishing his body. He would regularly collapse at home after a cycle.

He would train twice a day. Billy spent half his day trying to get the rest of us to train and the other half was spent trying to stop Larry. We had gym membership in Jury's and Billy would ask the lads there to stop Larry from going in.

This was the new world in which we would play football for Cork.

I loved it.

• • • • •

My life seemed to take on a degree of normality in 1987. I was out of the Under-21 grade so that meant I had four less teams to play with. I was also appointed captain of the Glanmire intermediate football team that year, something I regarded as a great honour. And then we started to draw nearly every Championship game we played in, in both football and hurling. It was the summer of draws and that meant that I would again be faced with a hectic and demanding schedule.

How about this for a summer of activity:

June 14, Munster senior hurling semi-final v Limerick (draw).

June 28, Munster senior hurling semi-final replay.

July 12, Munster senior hurling final v Tipperary (draw).

July 19, Munster senior hurling final replay.

July 26, Munster senior football final v Kerry (draw).

August 2, Munster senior football final replay.

Over eight Sundays, I played six major Championship games and those included four Munster finals on consecutive Sundays. As if that wasn't enough, we managed to draw the All-Ireland football semi-final with Galway.

My life revolved around training and playing. It was during those months of 1987 that I truly appreciated what people around me were facilitating. My colleagues at work were making sacrifices and taking on extra duties to allow me to meet my commitments. At home my mother was working all the hours she could, to ensure that I was always prepared for whatever was happening with Cork or the club.

As Munster and All-Ireland hurling champions there was a sharp focus on us that year, especially as we were attempting to defend those titles without Jimmy Barry Murphy. Adding further spice to the hurling Championship were the excited rumblings coming from the sleeping giant of hurling, Tipperary. Michael 'Babs' Keating had been appointed their team manager for the year and his big personality and the optimism he brought to the county after years in the wilderness created a new atmosphere.

Even back then, we were all fairly wary of too much exposure in the media. Babs had no such hang-ups. He created an aura about his Tipperary team and used the media to good effect. He was naturally talkative and helped to generate even greater interest in the Championship and especially in a meeting between Tipperary and Cork.

I was never really consulted about how I would train. Billy and Johnny seemed to reach an easy agreement. If the hurlers had a match coming up I trained with them and vice versa. I did what I was told and I was happy with that.

My Championship began with the hurlers against Limerick in Semple Stadium. It was my first time to play in Thurles and I liked it immediately. The ground wasn't full but there was a great atmosphere around the place. The lads had told me I would like the surface, and I did.

Limerick hadn't enjoyed much success since the early 1970s but they had produced a few good minor and Under-21 teams that were beginning to feed into the senior team. Gary Kirby was attracting a lot of attention and he was one of the youngest guys on an otherwise experienced team. Tommy Quaid was in goals, they had strong players like Pa Carey, Liam O'Donoghue, who marked me that day, Ger Hegarty, Jimmy Carroll, Shane Fitzgibbon and Paddy Kelly in the team.

Overall it proved to be a good day for me, though I did encounter a couple of problems. In the match programme my club was given as Bishopstown! I often wondered what Barry Coffey and Paul McGrath made of that. And I picked up a toe injury during the game that was a cause for concern in the days that followed. But I was told I played well in my first ever Munster hurling Championship game and I had scored my first senior Championship point. The game ended in a draw, 3-11 each.

The injury meant that I did not play for the footballers against Limerick the following Saturday night in the provincial semi-final. Larry and Shea did play for the first time in the Munster Championship and Cork won by six points.

I was back in action for the hurling replay, this time attached to the right club and wearing the No.10 jersey. John Fenton scored 1-8 and we were fairly comfortable winners by 3-14 to 0-10.

On July 12, I played in my first Munster senior hurling final. Tipperary had also qualified. It was in Thurles. As players we were isolated to a certain extent from the hype that was building up to the game. I didn't have anything to compare it with and I was so preoccupied with my own dual preparations that I didn't get over-anxious about the game. I was always fairly laidback anyway.

It was only when our team bus turned into Thurles that even the most experienced players sat up and took notice. It was a sunny day and the streets were thronged with supporters making their way to Semple Stadium. Outside the bars, and especially Hayes' Hotel, men and women, boys and girls, wearing the red and white of Cork or the blue and yellow of Tipperary gathered. As we passed, the Cork supporters cheered loudly.

We got to the ground in time for the minor game which also involved Cork and Tipperary and I remember the surprise felt by players and officials at the number of people already in the ground. In the end, an attendance of 56,000 was recorded but we learned later that thousands more gained free entry when two gates were broken down.

As a player I don't remember it as a great game, for us especially. But it has gone down as a classic. Tipperary played well and might have won it. But they could never get away from us and Kieran Kingston almost won it for us near the end with a goal. All the pressure of the day fell on the shoulders of Pat Fox when he stood over a free in the last minute to earn them a draw. He scored it and I don't think any of us were too disappointed. 'The Great Escape' was the headline in the *Examiner* and it didn't refer to Fox's late point. It reflected our play.

We went to Killarney for the replay seven days later. The venue was a controversial choice. Cork and Tipperary traditionally had an agreement about Championship fixtures that would have meant the replay took place in Pairc Ui Chaoimh. But the agreement had run out after the drawn game and Tipperary would not agree to start a new arrangement by travelling to our home venue.

Everyone suspected that Tipperary did not want to hand any sort of advantage to us and felt their young, inexperienced team would be better off at a neutral venue, if they could not get us to go to Thurles again. I found it all amusing. Grown men fighting like kids, they were. Anyway, I was delighted because Killarney was already high on my list of favourite grounds.

I played one of my best-ever games for the hurlers and if we had won the game I'm sure I would have won the Man of the Match award. I was flying at the time. In the week before the game I felt brilliant. I was jumping out of my skin. I told my pal (and future brother-in-law, though we didn't know that at the time) John O'Neill to bet £20 on me to win the award. I should have won it, too, and we should have won the match. It was one of the few occasions when I thought a refereeing decision denied us victory.

This was a completely different performance from us. We pummelled them from the start and were six points up before they seemed to realise the match was on. They seemed paralysed by the incredible noise in the stadium. Their supporters, starved of success and now excited at the prospects of the new team, had created an amazing atmosphere in Thurles. Our supporters responded in Killarney. The weather was lovely. It was the perfect setting.

We scored 1-10 in the first half but we should have had at least two more goals. Nicky English scored a typically opportunistic goal for them and we led by five points at half time and it should have been an awful lot more.

There were a number of controversial moments in the second half. They claimed that a Pat Fox shot that seemed to come back off the post had actually gone into the net, hit the stanchion at the back and come back into play. They scored a point off it. Maybe they were right. I have no doubt that we got a perfectly legitimate goal just afterwards that would have won the game for us.

I won a puck out from Ger Cunningham and drove it to the edge of the square where I knew Tony O'Sullivan was waiting. He flicked it to the net. The referee, Terence Murray, blew his whistle and signalled a free-out, suggesting Tony was in the square. He wasn't even bordering on the square. I was furious and am convinced to this day we would have won the game if the goal had been allowed.

Near the end of a frantic second half in which there was hardly time to draw a breath, we were leading by a point. English got possession and was bearing down on goal when he opted to go for a point. It meant extra time but, in reality, it won the game for them. They were a younger, fresher team. They lasted the extra 30 minutes much better than many of our players. It was a massive result for them because they hadn't won a Munster title since 1971. Michael Doyle had come on for extra time and scored two goals for Tipperary. They celebrated wildly while we withdrew quietly.

It was a proud but sad day for us. It was John Fenton's last Munster final. Tom Cashman played on for another year. I'm proud to say I was considered good enough to play on teams that contained such great players and men.

I hadn't time for such reflections then.

My thoughts turned immediately to Kerry.

CHAPTER**8**

REDEMPTION

It is amazing how a couple of minutes of injury time at the end of a football game can change lives and alter the course of sporting history.

Just a week after we had lost the 1987 Munster hurling final to Tipperary, I was playing for the footballers against Kerry. That July 26 would be our Redemption Day. We didn't win the game but we broke a psychological barrier that effectively shaped our futures.

It was the day we stood up for ourselves. Physically and mentally we imposed ourselves on Kerry. It was an announcement that we were no longer fearful or intimidated by their record, their skills or the colour of that jersey. It was the end of one era and the start of another in which Cork and not Kerry would be the dominant force.

Shea and I were partners in midfield for the first time that day. The team was taking a familiar shape. John Kerins was well established as our goalkeeper. Colman Corrigan was now a permanent fixture at full-back. Conor Counihan was at No.6, Larry at No.11 and the vastly experienced Christy Ryan was put in at full-forward.

Around those players, Billy and the selectors fitted in the talents of Tony Davis, Niall Cahalane, Tony Nation, Paddy Hayes, John O'Driscoll and John Cleary. They switched Jimmy Kerrigan into the attack. They rotated players like Barry Coffey, Danny Culloty, Tony Leahy, Colm O'Neill, Paul McGrath and Mick McCarthy.

There was some talk about Kerry reaching the end of an era. Certainly, some of their oldest players had been around for more than a decade but the likes of Paidi, Sean Walsh, Jack O'Shea, Pat Spillane, Mikey Sheehy, Bomber Liston and Ger Power were still intimidating opponents. It wasn't just their reputations that frightened those who faced them during those final years of their domination; they were still able to produce special moments, as we were to learn.

They had some younger players, too, like Tom Spillane and Ger Lynch who had picked up three All-Irelands in succession in the previous three Championships. We needed to beat them soon. They had not needed to play particularly well in the two previous Championship meetings between the teams to win. We had talked about the game, about our anxieties, why good Cork teams had been unable to match Kerry so often in the recent past.

It was important to recognise that Kerry had been blessed, that so many supremely talented footballers had come along at the same time and that Mick O'Dwyer proved so adept at creating a team from those individual talents. Their record between 1975 and 1986 was phenomenal. To win eight All-Ireland Championships in that period showed incredible consistency.

Having acknowledged that, we needed to look at ourselves. There was an abundance of talent in our own dressing room. What we needed to develop was self-belief. We didn't fear any other team in the country and we needed to cast aside any doubts we had about Kerry. What we needed to do, in short, was beat them.

We should have had them beaten on that sunny summer's day in The Park and we very nearly let them off the hook.

Normal time was completed and we led by two points, 1-9 to 1-7. Larry had already kicked seven points. John O'Driscoll had scored a goal in the first half. Bomber had been having a quiet game by his standards but still managed to get a goal before half time which kept them in the game.

Our lead should have been more. Ten scores was just not a good enough return. We were the better team; we knew it. There was a twenty-minute period in the second half when Kerry didn't score. Yet we couldn't put them away. The weight of modern history was crushing us. We knew if we got over this game that everything would change. Maybe that's why we made it so hard on ourselves.

They came at us hard.

Paidi took a free and drove it towards our goal. It broke over to the sideline where Ambrose O'Donovan got the ball and banged it back across in front of the square. Someone got a fist to it and it broke to the right.

A mad scramble ensued.

Michael McAuliffe and Mikey Sheehy exchanged hand-passes. Our defence was bamboozled. Barry Coffey and Denis Walsh ran into each other trying to get Sheehy. Sheehy danced and twisted past a couple of players and somehow squeezed the ball between Kerins and the near post.

Goal.

We were a point behind and time was up. Some heads went down. Billy lay prostrate on the ground in front of the stand, his face buried into the grass. He thought Kerry had broken our resolve and our hearts again, and couldn't face it. I turned to get back into position for the kick out. My back was to our goal so I didn't see what happened. John Kerins had reacted very quickly. He plucked the ball out of the net and had kicked it back outfield while Kerry players were still celebrating, and some of our lads were lamenting a fate that hadn't befallen them. Some of their players were protesting that the kick out had been taken too quickly. I was watching as Larry got the ball and laid it off to O'Driscoll. He was fouled and the referee, Pat Lane, signalled a free.

It was an incredible moment for Larry as he stood over that ball facing into the Blackrock end. This was his first Munster final and the fate of his adopted county and colleagues was in his hands. Or, at his feet to be more precise.

He started his run up and stopped. For a second I thought something was wrong. Then he just stepped back again, reset himself and took the free. His right foot did not let us down. The ball sailed over the bar. Charlie Nelligan didn't even have time to place the ball for the kick out. The referee held out his hands, blew the whistle. It was a draw.

You could sense a new mood in our dressing room. A few officials looked a bit despondent that we had not won the game. The fear of this Kerry team was deeply ingrained in Cork souls and they were immediately worried that we would not win a replay in Killarney.

As more and more players filed in, optimism began to grow.

We were all on a high.

"When is the replay?" someone shouted.

"Play it now!"

"We'll head for Killarney now."

"We don't need to wait a fucking week."

"We're ready now."

Billy was really fired up. He went around to every player, rousing us. Honestly, we were ready to go back out again and take them on. The despair that had followed Sheehy's goal was replaced by elation. I don't ever remember a dressing room like it after a game.

Everything had changed.

We felt it on the field. Individually we detected an alteration in status and only when we got together did we realise that it was a collective realisation. The tables had turned.

My own battle with O'Donovan was a case in point. I felt he was trying to physically intimidate me a couple of times. I was playing well, fielding balls above his head, catching everything. The next time a ball went over our heads, too high to contest, we began to follow the play. So did everyone else, that's why no one saw anything.

As I came from behind, I gave him a box in the face. That box delivered a message. I would not be messed around with. It is not something that I would advocate on a pitch but sometimes you have to do things to assert yourself. I think the message got through. I never had any real problem with Kerry afterwards. There was one incident a few years later but I was only one of many who joined in.

There were some comments in the days after the game about what had happened to O'Donovan. One Kerry official was quoted as saying that it was the worst incident he had ever seen on a football field. That was simply not true. No one saw it, not even the umpires, who were looking straight up the pitch. If they had seen it they would surely have reported me to the referee. And there was no reaction from the crowd or, more pertinently, the Kerry dug-out.

I don't know if the Kerry players discussed it afterwards. There certainly wasn't any evidence of a revenge mission a week later. I half expected to get a couple of clips early in the game but it never happened.

Did the Kerry players or their management accept that we were a new force in the week before the replay? By half time in Killarney they knew. They scored just one point in the first half. A forward line that contained the combined talents of John Kennedy, Jack O'Shea, Pat Spillane, Mikey Sheehy, Eoin Liston and Ger Power managed just one score between them.

We had scored seven.

We were completely on top. Power was sent off just before half time and that really finished it. We won by 0-13 to 1-5 and the only criticism of us was that we didn't win the game by more.

It was a strange game. Eight of our players scored, including myself, chipping in with a point. Tony Davis got two wearing No.2 though he was our spare man after Power was sent off and had a licence to roam. Tony Nation also scored. Our defenders were not known for getting on the score-sheet. Their goal came late in the game. Jacko had a couple of chances for goals but had to settle for points. We were never fearful of losing though we continued to make life just a little harder for ourselves than we needed to.

In the stands and on the terraces in Fitzgerald Stadium I know our supporters remained fearful until the final whistle. My brothers made me promise not to put them through such torture again. We hadn't learned how to put teams away. But on the field I don't think we had any doubts, even when our lead was cut to four points. Our mentality had changed. We were cautious but less fearful.

It was a massive victory for lots of reasons. Our confidence soared. In fact we got over-confident for a short while and nearly suffered the consequences on our first visit to Croke Park a couple of weeks later. But we never feared Kerry again and we would dominate them for the best part of the next ten years.

It was important for Billy also because he had proven himself as a coach. In his first season he had put together a team that could beat Kerry. Remember, it was only Cork's second Munster title since Billy himself had won his last one as a player, in 1974. He had suffered so much heartbreak against Kerry that this was a significant triumph. He never displayed a lack of confidence, except in that moment the week before when Sheehy got his goal, but this must have been a great psychological boost to him.

It is impossible to say what might have happened if we had not drawn the first game. Billy and the selectors, the county board even, had taken big risks, especially bringing Larry and Shea on board. A lot of questions would have been asked and some heads could have rolled. Billy wasn't always the most popular man with some on the committee, and his opponents would surely have fired a few shots his way.

I still think we would have gone on to win an All-Ireland title in the future because of the amount of talent available. But it might have been a far rockier road.

Of course, we nearly made a complete mess of the year two weeks later. We trained for the All-Ireland semi-final but our heads were elsewhere. Were we still basking in the glory of beating Kerry? I don't know. We were raging-hot favourites to beat Galway in the semi-final and we were blessed to get a draw. It was the biggest fright we got in all our years at the top level, even bigger than our reaction to Sheehy's late strike a few weeks earlier.

For some reason Galway came in under the radar. They had lot of players who had played in the infamous 1983 final, with loads of experience: Seamus McHugh, Tomas Tierney, Brian Talty, Val Daly, Barry Brennan, Gay McManus, Brian O'Donnell and Stephen Joyce were still around. We were good enough to win the game at our best but we should never have underestimated them. They deserved to win.

Talty and Hugh Blehein faced Shea and myself. They made life difficult for us. I can't explain our lethargy. I wondered later if I was paying the price for having played so many competitive and energy-sapping matches in Munster. I was young and very fit but they must have taken a toll.

We started well but then let them back into the game. Val Daly scored a goal for them before half time and generally troubled us with his play. John Kerins made two good saves in the second half that kept us in the game. Twice we had led by four or more points but, as the game went into injury time, we were a point behind and facing elimination. I remember watching their corner-back, John Fallon, give them the lead and fearing that we had wasted all the hard work that had gone into beating Kerry.

Larry had been struggling with a hamstring problem ever since the Munster final. You wouldn't have known it when he stood up to another crucial last-minute free that day in Croke Park. It was a long-range one. He placed the ball about fifty-three yards from the Galway goal. All I can remember is the height he put on the ball and the power of the kick. If there hadn't been netting at the Hill 16 end he would have kicked the ball out of the ground. It was incredible.

We won the replay easily, 0-18 to 1-4. Larry kicked points for fun, eleven altogether. We missed at least two clear-cut chances for goals. There was simply no comparison between the two teams. It should never have needed a replay. And a replay was the last thing I needed after the series of draws in Munster.

We dominated midfield that day. I felt much better and was happier with my display. Galway brought in a substitute at midfield that day, a lad named Noel Mannion. He only played for twenty minutes but I remembered him. Two years later I was watching the Ireland versus Wales rugby International from Cardiff. This big lad wearing the No.8 jersey for Ireland made a great block as a Welsh player attempted to chip the ball through the Irish line. The Irish No.8 held onto the ball. He then ran sixty or seventy yards with half the Welsh team in pursuit.

Like most Irish people watching him I was on my feet roaring. It was only after he scored a brilliant try and was getting up that I realised who it was – Noel Mannion again. This time I was on his side.

For the second year in a row, I had a September date in Croke Park. It was becoming an annual feature. I was also about to encounter another team wearing green, with a tint of gold, who would play a huge part in my career and in the fate of that Cork football team.

We were about to be introduced to Meath for the first time.

CHAPTER**9**

TACKLING MEATH

If there was as much bad blood between Cork and Meath footballers in the late 1980s as history suggests, then how come I didn't taste any of it?

That might seem a strange question to people who followed that period or who have read about it since. I suspect there might be a few of the Meath lads who will be taken aback by it. But I never felt any real enmity towards the Meath players. I don't reflect on our rivalry with any bitterness at all.

It would be inaccurate to suggest that there was sweet harmony between us. You don't get sweet harmony on a football field. There were hard belts given and taken and some of the belts that Meath and Cork players gave each other had great force behind them.

Was it any worse than anything I experienced over the years with Kerry? I honestly have to say no. There were stories of squabbles off the field between players at various functions and on a holiday when the two squads found themselves staying in the same hotel in the Canary Islands. It all went over my head. I never had any problems with the Meath lads. I got to know Mick Lyons in Australia, in 1986. He was, and is, one of the nicest guys you could meet. Of course, he was tough on the field.

Weren't we all, at times?

He gave me a couple of clatters over the years that I didn't appreciate. And I got belts from a few other Meath players. I didn't hold back myself. It was the way we played the game. Football is physical. You go on the field expecting big collisions. A football field, especially for big Championship games, is not for the faint-hearted. That was part of the attraction for me as a player and used to be part of the attraction when I became a supporter again.

Whatever happened on the field stayed there, as far as I was concerned. Maybe I didn't always feel the same way about games involving Kerry! Anyway, if games between Cork and Meath were so rough, how come only two players were sent off in the course of four different finals between 1987 and 1990? Yes, there were a couple of League games that were spicy, to say the least, but I never bought into the notion that the teams hated each other.

Through all the years I played both football and hurling for Cork I never experienced any real tension against any team, other than Kerry. The history between Kerry and Cork goes back to the 19th century. In hurling during that era a rivalry did build against Tipperary but it never got out of control. And I honestly don't believe our rivalry with Meath was out of control at any time.

In my mind, two counties need to have a long history with each other to build up what amounts to hatred. And there was no history between Cork and Meath, apart from the fact that the two counties had met in an All-Ireland final in 1967, twenty years before we met in 1987 and just two years after I was born.

Billy played in that final. So, too, did one of the Meath selectors, Pat Reynolds. But we were never aware of any problems between those two teams.

In 1987, it was new to all the players. Croke Park was like a second home to Meath but this group of players had never played in an All-Ireland final. In that respect, I was the most experienced player on the field having won the hurling title just a year before. I have no doubt it helped my preparation. I was calm and controlled through the build-up and on the morning of the game.

There was already talk about joining the list of players who had won All-Ireland senior medals in football and hurling. At that stage of my career it was not something that bothered me at all. I was 22 and was looking ahead to years of opportunities. It was the advantage of being born in Cork.

At an early stage in the final, it seemed as if I was well on my way to becoming a member of the illustrious elite. We were flying. Meath were struggling to get into the game. We went five points up, 0-7 to 0-2. It should have been at least three points more.

For one Meath kick out I was standing a little adrift of a group of players.

Their goalkeeper, Mickey McQuillan, tried to put distance as well as height on his kick. I timed everything well. Waiting for the ball to start dropping I took a couple of steps before launching myself into the air.

It was one of the times when I could almost feel myself floating. I scaled the lads in front of me, teammates and opponents, and plucked the ball out of the sky and landed running. Jimmy Kerrigan appeared at my side. I passed it off to him. He headed towards goal. Mick Lyons stepped forward. I screamed at Jimmy for a pass.

He went for his score.

Lyons was brilliant in those one-on-ones. He stood his ground and timed a block perfectly. The chance was gone. "If I was a fucking Nemo man you would have passed it," I told him later. I was certain I would have got a goal.

The ball went back down the pitch. There was a bit of a scramble in front of our goal. I think Kerinsy made a save, the ball broke and Colm O'Rourke stuck out a hand and pushed the ball into the net. It wasn't the best goal Colm ever scored but it turned out to be one of the most important. We had been, by far, the better team in that first half yet we went back to the dressing room at half time a point behind, 0-8 to 1-6. I still felt good about the game. We had played the better football and we just needed to keep doing that. The problem was that our performance levels fell and theirs improved.

The tension certainly heightened in the second half. I remember seeing Billy racing onto the pitch at one stage, in a rage over something. Gerry McEntee and himself had a few words. I didn't hear them but I don't think they were praying. Our forwards had been flying in the first half but we couldn't buy a score in the second. We scored just three points in 35 minutes. It wasn't good enough. Meath had six points to spare at the end. We couldn't complain.

In the wake of an All-Ireland defeat we might have expected some kind of fall-out. In fact, it just petered out. I think the fact that we had won a Munster title, laid the Kerry ghost to rest and qualified for an All-Ireland final satisfied people. That's not normally the way in Cork, but there is no doubt we had made substantial progress in a year. Anyway, we were all far too busy to dwell on the game.

I was captain of the Glanmire intermediate team. I was also playing for Imokilly. And I was playing for Sarsfields in the Cork hurling Championship.

We were still lagging behind the other big hurling clubs in Cork at the time but we were improving, getting stronger every year.

The year ended with Glanmire winning the county intermediate Championship. I was in midfield, Denis played in goal. In its own way on a local level it was as big as an All-Ireland triumph. The pride in the faces of the older members of the club told us what it meant to them.

I have a picture in my mind of Tim Nyhan walking through the village with the cup in his hand, minding it carefully. It meant more to him than the Sam Maguire. Denis and myself were getting a lift from Liam Hederman. As we drove up to Tim, I ordered Liam to slow down. I climbed out the window, perching myself precariously on the door and, as we passed Tim, I tried to grab the cup. Tim nearly collapsed with the fright but he held onto the cup.

Imokilly reached the county senior football final again. Facing us were Nemo – Jimmy Kerrigan, Tony Nation, Shea, Dinny Allen and a kid named Steven O'Brien, amongst their players. They beat us 2-11 to 0-9. It was a decent showing from Imokilly because we got very little time to train together that summer with Cork reaching the All-Ireland final and Glanmire tied up the whole year with the intermediate Championship.

You hear a lot of talk these days about burnout and the need for a closed season. I didn't have time to feel burned out. My feet might have been blistered and sore from all the football and hurling I was playing, but I never got a break. Remember, the National Leagues started in October at that time. The coaches were careful with me but I was still back in action with both the Cork hurlers and footballers within weeks of the football final. There was no end to the season.

Sometimes today, I get amused listening to all the talk about training methods, all these heavy weights being lifted. I was doing the right sort of training back then. I was playing games all the time. I didn't need training. I needed a rest.

•••••

Anyone looking for bad blood between ourselves and another team didn't have to look too far, certainly not as far as Meath. You only had to picture the border between Cork and Kerry to imagine some of that blood being spilled in 1988.

I'm not sure what caused it. Maybe they were a team in decline and were finding it hard to accept they could no longer beat Cork on a whim. And possibly we were still nervous against Kerry, still just a little spooked by the sight of the green and gold.

With Conor Counihan and Jack O'Shea the central figures in the early physical exchanges in Pairc Ui Chaoimh there were certainly mysterious forces at work.

Conor and Jacko were two tough, hard footballers. I knew both of them very well at that stage, having spent four weeks in Australia with Jacko, in 1986. Off the field they were two mild-mannered men, good company. You wouldn't describe them as shrinking violets on the field but you wouldn't expect them to be at the centre of any trouble.

The build-up to the Munster final that year was confusing. Kerry had battered Waterford in the semi-final, as expected. We went to Askeaton to play Limerick and were lucky to get out of it with a three-point win. It was a chaotic day. I remember one official, not part of the selection committee, roaring at us before the game about Cork's traditional supremacy over Limerick and that we should, "keep the ball low".

He thought it was a hurling game.

We were terrible.

I was terrible, starting at full-forward for the first time. Billy took me off. It was the first time in the Championship that I was pulled from the fray because I was playing badly. It only happened once more and that is a story for later. We won by three points, 0-9 to 1-3. Larry kicked six of those points. It was a bad day. Tommy Sugrue from Kerry was the referee. We would meet again later in the year, when it would be another bad day.

Dinny Allen had been coaxed back into the squad. Dave Barry was also back. He had spent a few years playing soccer with Cork City and had not been selected for Cork. They must both have wondered that day if they had made a mistake returning.

I missed the post-mortems. Hurling duty beckoned for myself and Denis Walsh and we were spared Billy's reaction in training. We had a big win over Clare, 3-22 to 2-9, in the first round. That meant another battle with Tipperary in the Munster final.

Before that there was a date with Kerry in the football final. We were back in The Park on July 3. It rained heavily before the game. Another torrential shower fell during the first half. Ambrose O'Donovan and myself were kept apart. He played at centre-back that day. Dermot Hanafin partnered Jacko against myself and Shea.

A lot of the focus before the game was on the Kerry subs bench. Sitting side by side in their green and navy tracksuits, were Eoin 'Bomber' Liston, Denis 'Ogie' Moran, Paidi O Se and Ger Power. Between them they held 31 All-Ireland senior football Championship medals.

We had a new kid in our team. Steven O'Brien started his first Championship game that day and you would have sworn he had been around for years, he was so calm and relaxed about it all. They had a new kid as well.

A lad named Maurice Fitzgerald.

We had seen him as a minor. There was a lot of talk about him in Munster. Now, here he was playing in his first senior final and all the talk was justified. He kicked ten points, seven of them from frees. Kerry scored a total of sixteen. The guy was pure class.

Dinny Allen scored a goal for us in the middle of the second half. We were the better team but Maurice Fitz kept Kerry in the game. There were just two points between us with only a few minutes left and the tension was rising. The Cork supporters amongst the 40,000 or so in the ground were getting nervous and the Kerry crowd was growing excited.

Two of the subs they threw on were Ger Power and the Bomber. Each arrival was greeted with an almighty roar. There was another roar from the crowd with about eight minutes to go. I didn't know what caused it. I turned around and saw Counihan lying on the ground. Pat Lane was the referee again and spoke to his umpires. They saw nothing.

Do officials ever see anything?

The game went on without any action being taken. Time was up and I remember Jacko getting the ball. Counihan tackled him hard. Lane awarded a free. The next thing I saw was Jacko getting involved. The players closest to them jumped in. I saw Bomber and Ambrose charge in. *Fuck this*, I said to myself. I went in as well. I think only Kerinsy and Charlie Nelligan stayed out of it.

I wouldn't say there was a decent punch thrown. There was a lot of pulling and dragging but there were so many players involved you hadn't room to swing a fist. It probably looked terrible but, in reality, it wasn't that bad. When we all calmed down Maurice kicked the free. Kerinsy kicked the ball out and the match ended. We won by 1-14 to 0-16. I immediately forgot about the row. There was no problem between the players. Certainly, a few Kerry lads shook hands with me before they left the field and we were presented with the cup.

The following day the controversy began. The row had been mentioned on TV on Sunday night. The newspapers had been indignant about our so-called 'behaviour'. The GAA authorities decided they had to act.

There was an investigation.

A gang of us were summoned to a meeting of the Munster Council, in Mallow. The newspapers were full of it. There was condemnation and indignation. I thought it was all a bit over the top. I was back training with the hurlers and Jim Cashman was giving me plenty of slagging.

"You should be getting ready to box in the Olympics," he would shout. "There's a medal out there in Seoul for ya."

Thanks, Jim.

Sections of the referee's report were published in the media. The referee wrote about what had happened after Conor's 'tackle' on Jacko. "I awarded a free to Kerry and booked Conor Counihan for the said foul and severely reprimanded him. While placing the ball I noticed a fracas between a number of players. Not having seen the start of this and having restored order on the field I decided to take no further action."

The two county committees were fined £300 each because of the conduct of their players; Cork was fined a further £100 "for continued unauthorised incursions on the field" by Billy. Myself, Steven O'Brien, Counihan, Jacko, Bomber, Morgan Nix, Ambrose and Joe Shannon were warned about our future conduct.

No, my wrist did not hurt from that slap.

What hurt a fortnight later was my pride. Tipperary beat us in the Munster hurling final, 2-19 to 1-13. At one stage during that game, we were being well beaten by twelve points but we fought and fought furiously to get back into the game. We brought the margin back to two points but the effort took a huge toll. Then big Cormac Bonnar was brought into the Tipp forward line and quickly scored a goal. That buried us. We did go down fighting. That was something.

•••••

I remember sitting down for a meal in Jury's Hotel on the Western Road in Cork towards the end of September, in 1988. The hotel is gone now. It was our headquarters. We would use the gym, go for a swim and talk football.

This was in the week after we had drawn with Meath in the All-Ireland football final. It was an informal session, guys just offering opinions about how the game went and making suggestions about what changes we might make for the replay which was scheduled for October 10.

There were nights when I tuned out of these exercises. I often kept my own counsel. I would chat to Billy about things. Bob Honohan and I were close and we would discuss issues. In the wider environment I tended to be a bit quieter. As this particular evening progressed I began to tune in more. It was the negative stuff that was getting under my skin. Some of our forwards were complaining about the rough treatment they were getting from the Meath backs. They were giving out about the type of ball going in. They were looking for support.

I thought, Fuck these guys... What's wrong with them?

Myself and Shea and Larry are out there being belted by Hayes. When we get away from him we're being met by McEntee. And if we manage to avoid him, Harnan is fucking waiting. And they're complaining about the kind of ball going in?

And looking for help?

They should deal with it themselves!

They should be damn glad we're getting any ball to them. Why don't they just get on with it and stop whingeing?

I did keep those thoughts to myself and maybe it was just as well.

We had beaten Monaghan well in the All-Ireland semi-final. Their goalkeeper, Paddy Linden, had made a few great saves that day, including one from me that prevented what would have been a rare Championship goal.

I did get a rare goal in the final against Meath and we should have won that game. We were the better team, no question about it, but we were denied by a bad refereeing decision from Tommy Sugrue in the last minute that gave Meath a second chance. Okay, you can argue that if we were the best team we should have been more than a point ahead. But you have to take into account that there was very little separating Cork and Meath at the time. We were the two best teams in Ireland and games between us were always tight affairs.

The drawn '88 final was one of the tightest of all. It and the replay were the reason why people said there was bad blood. I think it was all exaggerated by some of the players, by the media and by the fact that the President of the GAA at the time, John Dowling, condemned some of the incidents in the replay.

Anyway, back to my goal.

I didn't get many in my career so it has to be recorded. The game was only a few minutes old and I had wandered up near the Meath goal. Dinny Allen sent in a lovely cross, I got the ball and squeezed it under Mickey McQuillan's legs and into the net. It was rare and wonderful. Larry took over from there and played brilliantly. He ended up with eight points. Only Michael McCarthy and myself managed to score for Cork as well.

We were a point ahead at the end of normal time. Sugrue played some injury time. We had no problem with that. Then a ball broke loose near our goal. Barry Coffey tried to shield it. David Beggy fell over. There wasn't even contact in my opinion. Sugrue whistled for a free. We went ballistic at what we felt was a terrible decision. Brian Stafford kicked a point. He could have done it with his eyes closed.

I have never been so annoyed over a refereeing decision. I was angry when Terence Murray had disallowed Tony's goal in the Munster hurling final the previous year, but this decision made me even more furious. That was a game we were entitled to win.

Meath were certainly more physical in the replay. Various players have admitted that since. They felt we had bullied them in the drawn game, that some of their players had taken heavy blows that were probably questionable.

The worst thing that could have happened to us was Gerry McEntee being sent off after seven minutes in the replay. He had given Niall Cahalane a box in the mouth straight in front of the referee.

I had a sinking feeling then. I hated a player being sent off against us. Instead of feeling like you're playing against fourteen men it actually feels like you're playing against sixteen. The other players up their game, they seem to find new sources of energy. The team that loses a player can galvanise itself. I remember, when I saw Gerry hit Niall, saying a quick prayer that he wouldn't be sent off.

I was pleased with my own display that day but I don't think we ever looked like winning. There was only a point in it at the end, 0-12 to 0-13, but we had cut it down from four in the last few minutes before time ran out. There was no immediate controversy about the game. Some Meath supporters didn't behave when they ran onto the pitch. Larry was the chief subject of their ire and he got a box from someone. I've often wondered how it didn't happen much more at the end of games when supporters were allowed to charge onto the field.

Then, the following day, John Dowling said he wasn't happy and that he would deal with it later. We had lost so it didn't matter to us. We were dealing with our disappointment in the time-honoured fashion with a few pints, and the comments of an official didn't disturb us. But the Meath lads felt it took a bit of the gloss off their win and some of them refused to accept their All-Ireland medals from Dowling later that year.

Many tales have circulated since then about relations between the Meath and Cork players. Coincidentally, we were booked into the same hotel in the Playa Del Ingles resort in Gran Canaria, the following January. I've heard stories about players avoiding each other, refusing to get into lifts together and all that. All I can say is that I had no problem with the Meath lads. I remember chatting to some of them on that trip. They can vouch for that.

I was sick of the sight of them on the football field, though. They had beaten us twice now in finals. But, that winter, I was more convinced than ever that this Cork team would win an All-Ireland. With the exception of Meath, there wasn't a team around who could compare with us. An All-Ireland was our destiny.

I truly believed that.

September of 1990 was the sweetest month in the history of Cork GAA, as Tomas Mulcahy and Larry Tompkins got to 'swap' the Liam MacCarthy and Sam Maguire Cups in front of a roaring crowd in Cork city centre. For Teddy McCarthy, the dual victory marked him as the only man in the lifespan of the GAA to win All-Ireland football and hurling medals in the one year.

Teddy finally got to play in the red shirt with his old North Mon school-mate, Tomas Mulcahy, joining legends like John Fenton and Jimmy Barry Murphy in Croke Park, chasing All-Ireland titles.

Tom Cashman raises the Liam MacCarthy Cup high after Cork's victory over Galway in the 1986 All-Ireland final – Teddy's first All-Ireland appearance.

The Cork team which defeated Galway in the 1986 All-Ireland final.

Johnny Clifford (top) showed incredible understanding in selecting Teddy for the 1986 All-Ireland hurling victory, while Fr Michael O'Brien proved just as astute in guiding the county to the title in 1990.

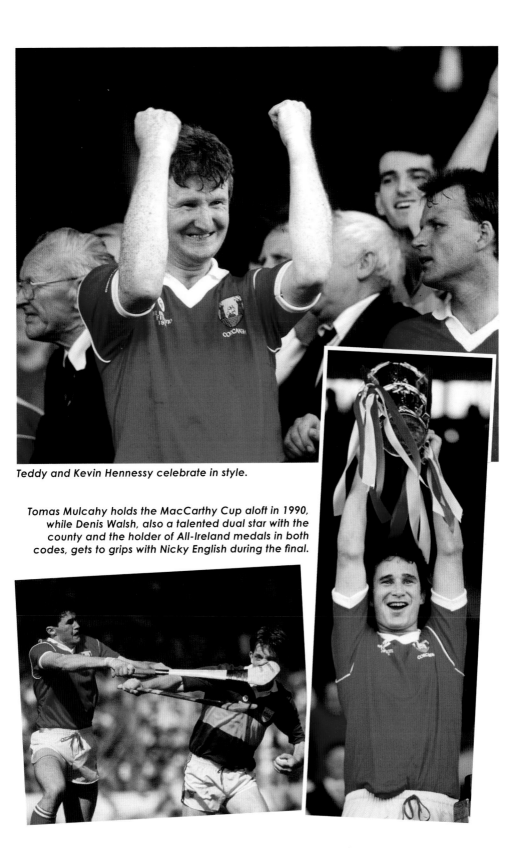

Teddy and Kevin Hennessy celebrate in style.

Tomas Mulcahy holds the MacCarthy Cup aloft in 1990, while Denis Walsh, also a talented dual star with the county and the holder of All-Ireland medals in both codes, gets to grips with Nicky English during the final.

The Cork team which defeated Tipperary in the 1990 All-Ireland hurling final.

Teddy seeks to break through the challenge of Kilkenny's Bill Hennessy in the 1992 All-Ireland final.

The Cork team which lost to Kilkenny in the 1992 All-Ireland final.

Kerry looked and felt unbeatable in
Cork's presence for so long, as the
likes of Jack O'Shea and Pat Spillane
(top) dominated Gaelic football;
Sean Walsh was a tower of strength
at full-back, and when Tommy
Doyle lifted the Sam Maguire in 1986
it looked as though their reign in
Munster might never come to an end.

Despite the controversial headlines, Teddy never found the battles with Meath in the late 1980s to be as tough or personal as those he experienced while going toe-to-toe with Kerry in Munster.

Billy Morgan brought new life into the Cork football team and, even though his famous 'finger' often meant bad news for some players, he was always there to support his team.

Larry Tompkins showed courage and composure under pressure which helped guide Cork to unprecedented success in the late '80s and early '90s.

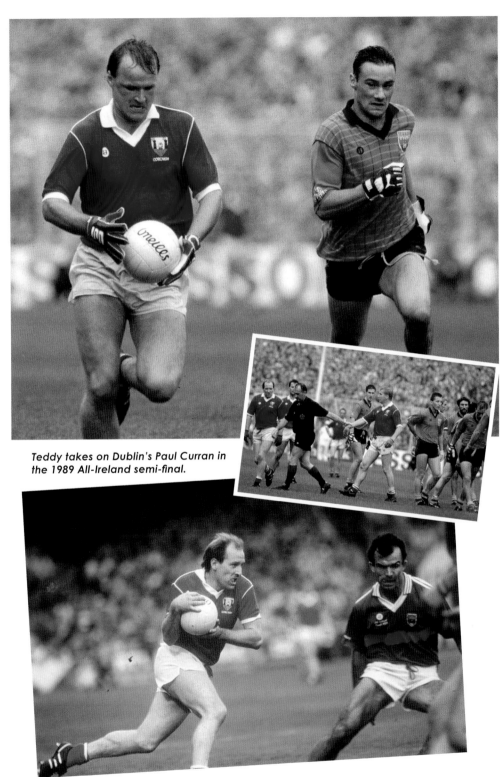

Teddy takes on Dublin's Paul Curran in the 1989 All-Ireland semi-final.

Dinny Allen and Dave Barry brought such dash and scoring ability to the Cork team when they received Billy's call in 1988.

The Cork team which defeated Mayo in the 1989 All-Ireland football final.

The Cork team which retained the All-Ireland title by beating old enemy, Meath, in 1990.

Larry Tompkins lifts the Sam Maguire Cup.

Tony Davis, one of the cleanest footballers of the Billy Morgan era, gets his marching orders in the tempestuous 1993 All-Ireland final against Derry.

Joe Kavanagh celebrates a scorching goal in the 1993 final, which was tight and closely contested to the end.

Frank Murphy – whom Teddy regarded as a rock for Cork players – with Cork Chairman, Jerry O'Sullivan, in 2009.

The Gerald McCarthy management team – and Teddy, who acted as a selector to the Cork manager – had to face astonishing demands from the county's hurlers to resign.

Teddy with Bertie Og Murphy who also felt the staggering pressure of player power.

Teddy's introduction to inter-county management with Laois, in 2012, was short and not altogether successful, but he came away from the experience with an even greater desire to prove himself on the sideline, perhaps someday with the Cork hurling team.

CHAPTER**10**

LOST AND FOUND

Everybody loves New York.

The Empire State Building, Central Park, Broadway and Times Square. Yellow cabs.

I went there for the first time in 1989 and I didn't like the place at all.

That wasn't a good reason to go missing. Neither was it the time or place to incur the wrath of Mr Billy Morgan. I did both.

What turned out to be one of the best years of my life did not have an auspicious start. Once again I conspired, of my own volition, to make a complete mess of the opportunities afforded to me, and came through unscathed.

I had won an All-Ireland football medal and joined an elite club; I had won an All Star award. And, better than all of those combined, I met Oonagh.

Before all of that, I had to contend with the culture shock that was New York. To celebrate the 75th anniversary of the GAA in the city, in 1989, the GAA had agreed to a request to stage a National Football League 'Away' final in the city's old Irish corner known as Gaelic Park, between New York and the winners of the 'Home' final. The final would be played over two legs, on May 7 and 14.

It wasn't something that had occupied our thoughts the previous winter as we recovered from the disappointment of losing to Meath again. We were playing in the relative anonymity of Division Two in the League and actually lost our first game to Mayo. We then went on a good run, won five games and drew one with Roscommon in The Park to qualify for the knock-out stages.

That was when the first talk of New York began. Billy had spent some time working there just a few years before. Larry had also worked there. Danny Culloty still had traces of his American accent, though I don't know which part of the place he came from!

We beat Armagh in the quarter-final; comfortably accounted for Kerry in the semi-final and then faced Dublin in the 'Home' final. It was our first time to face this Dublin team. Many of them had won an All-Ireland title six years earlier and had played in the finals of 1984 and '85. Like ourselves, they had spent two seasons in the shadow of Meath but there was a general view at the time that they could become Championship contenders. We intended keeping them firmly subdued.

I was flying. Larry and myself were in midfield against Dublin and we enjoyed ourselves. I kicked three points in the first half and that was the margin we won by in the end. We survived a late scare when a Barney Rock attempt for a goal came back off the post.

It was time to get out the passports, and pack our bags. There was also plenty of company on the trip. The Galway hurlers, as All-Ireland champions, would play the hurling All Stars in an exhibition game as part of the Gaelic Park presentation. I knew most of them by then, and expected I would spend some time in their company on the twelve-day trip. The mood was light. We had a title to play for but it was more like heading off on a holiday than a competitive game.

Billy had sensed that holiday mood in the build up. He brought us together a couple of days before we left for New York and had some wise words along the lines of, "Let's get this over and done with on the first day and we can enjoy ourselves for the rest of the trip." It was sound advice.

New York had some decent footballers who were known to us. Martin Connolly had won an All-Ireland Under-21 medal with Cork in 1981 on a team that included Colman Corrigan and Dave Barry. Padraig Dunne was at midfield on the Offaly team that had stopped Kerry's bid for five All-Ireland titles in a row in 1982. Aidan Wiseman had been a respected player with Louth, as had Eunan McIntyre (Donegal), JP O'Kane (Antrim), John Owens

(Tipperary) and Vinny Hatton (Wicklow). Also playing for them was my old pal from Carlow, Willie Doyle, whom I hadn't seen since we were in Australia together.

I was looking forward to the trip. For a guy who had never left Ireland before August of 1986, I had already visited Australia and now I was on my way to another continent. I was getting used to airports and the hustle and bustle of international travel. I had also arranged to meet some old school friends in New York and I was looking forward to that.

I remember the journey from Kennedy Airport into Manhattan. The skyline was impressive. The traffic wasn't. I had seen New York traffic jams on TV shows but the reality was even worse. My mood darkened at an early stage. We were staying at a hotel called the Penta on 7th Avenue, just across the road from Madison Square Garden. The New York Knicks basketball team was playing the Boston Celtics in a big NBA game in the Garden, and our own basketball players, John O'Driscoll and Danny Culloty, were gushing with enthusiasm.

I'm afraid I didn't have enthusiasm for much after the first night. I couldn't settle. It was the smell coming from the sewers, the constant noise, sirens blasting from fire engines and ambulances and cop cars, people rushing all the time.

I'm told New York has been cleaned up since those days. It needed to be. 42nd Street was a couple of blocks away and it was a dump. We were warned to stay away from it at night. It is supposed to be a nice spot now, really fashionable. That is hard to imagine. It was rundown; there was rubbish everywhere, people lurking in doorways and in alleys. There was supposed to be an Irish pub beside the hotel. We went in. It was dark and grimy. There were shamrocks on the wall and a picture of John F. Kennedy. But that was about the only Irish connection I could see.

I was rooming with Colm O'Neill and I'd say he was fed up with my moaning by the time we were getting ready to go to Gaelic Park on the Sunday. Colm and I knew each other well by that time. We had played against each other many times at under-age level and then played at all the grades for Cork. He was trying to cheer me up but it wasn't easy. The game was a welcome distraction. I played well enough and we won by seven points, 1-12 to 1-5.

Deep down we knew after the game that the second leg should be a formality.

John O'Neill, my old teammate from school and good friend, was working in Boston at the time and he had come to New York for the game. I always enjoy John's company, even though, at that time, he was keeping a secret from me, something to which I will return. We had good fun. He was confident moving around the city and I felt good in his company. When he was heading back to Boston I felt lost.

Billy could see I wasn't happy. I had been moody around the hotel and he asked me what was wrong. I told him that I would like to spend a few days in Boston with John. He agreed.

"Get back here by Friday," he told me.

And I did.

But that was when the trouble started. I had a few drinks on Friday night. Then on Saturday I met a friend, named JJ. We went a bit mad. I ended up staying the night in his apartment somewhere outside Manhattan. We had no idea of the time when we woke on Sunday morning. I thought about the game. A little panic began to set in. My gear was back at the hotel.

"There's no way we'll get all the way into Manhattan, collect the gear and then get to the Bronx in time," JJ told me. I smelled trouble immediately.

I wondered would Colm think of bringing the gear.

No, he wouldn't, I decided.

We rang the hotel but the bus had already left. There was nothing left to do. We had to get to the Penta, get the gear and get to Gaelic Park as quickly as possible.

After a hair-raising journey from one borough of New York to another, JJ double-parked on 7th Avenue as I ran into the hotel to get my bag. The place was busy and the lift seemed to take ages. I was panting by the time I got to my room.

No bag.

Colm had brought it with him.

Luckily, JJ had brought some gear with him. It wasn't in the pristine condition my mother would have sent me out in. The togs were so old they had gone yellow. The socks were the old heavy woollen type, the boots were rugby boots. And they were packed into a plastic bag with the name of a grocer emblazoned on it.

When we eventually arrived at Gaelic Park I thought I was in good time. It was unlikely that the selectors would allow me to start but at least I would be part of the squad. I arrived at the stiles and explained who I was.

Yer man was unimpressed.

"I'm playing today," I pleaded with him.

"I don't care who you say you are, if you don't pay ten dollars like everyone else you won't be coming in here today."

Having parted with the money I tried to sneak into the ground without being noticed. Some chance. The team was already warming up. I had mistaken the time. The game was starting at 2.30pm, not 3pm. It had something to do with broadcast times back in Ireland. Over 5,000 people were packed into the place. It was hopping. Some people in the crowd spotted me and the jeering started.

I ran into the dressing room but couldn't find my bag. There were 27 or 28 bags lying on the floor and they all looked exactly the same. I hadn't time to go rifling through them to see which contained my gear.

I tried one or two.

They were full of street clothes.

The clock was ticking. So, I put on the old duds and ran out to the gate to join the rest of the lads on the field. The gate man looked me up and down. He wasn't impressed and wouldn't open up. I didn't have a pass and the teams were already out. He wouldn't relent no matter what I said to him.

Bob Honohan had been looking out for me and spotted me at the gate. He came over but the guy on the gate was insistent. I wasn't getting in unless I could produce a pass.

Bob went to Billy.

I could see him pointing at me.

Then, above the din of the crowd, I heard Billy say, "Leave the fucker there!" As he walked away my heart sank. Eventually, Bob got me in. My walk down the sideline in front of the old rickety stand was the loneliest I ever made.

What I had also forgotten was that the match was being broadcast live on RTÉ back home. In his commentary, Micheal O Muircheartaigh had mentioned that I was no longer on the team-sheet and something about me not being in the ground. The lads at home were watching the TV and soon the word went round that I was missing.

"Teddy is lost in New York," was the story.

I think it was said that I had been kidnapped, that they were afraid I had been dumped in the river. I was out there somewhere in the big, bad world, all alone. A phone call to my mother later allayed those fears.

As the game began I moved down the sideline nearer the goals, at the end of the field furthest from the dressing rooms and, more importantly, further away from Billy. He hadn't even looked at me. It meant that I was right in line with the most controversial incident on the field.

The game hadn't been on that long and Cork were attacking. I heard a roar, obviously of pain, and I looked. Colman Corrigan was on the ground and in agony. There was no one near him. Willie Doyle was about five yards away. I didn't know what had happened. In fact, Colman had ruptured his Achilles tendon and thought he had been kicked. Willie was closest and the finger of blame was pointed. I felt sorry for Willie but there was nothing I could do.

Cork won the game 2-9 to 1-9.

The League title was safe. The mood around the camp was dark. Colman had gone to hospital. Players were angry. Billy was fuming. Colman and Billy were close. Billy was mad at everyone – New York, Willie Doyle. And me.

Mick McCarthy and myself got out of there quickly and headed for a local bar. Some of the New York players arrived in. Willie Doyle was with them. About half an hour later Billy arrived. He made a beeline for Willie.

I said to Mick, "I'm going over there. Willie's a good guy and Billy has got to know that Willie is not responsible for what happened."

"Sit down, you clown," said Mick. "The last man in the world that should go over there is you. If Morgan sees you then Willie Doyle won't have a thing to worry about. Now, let's get out of here before he sees you." We swiftly finished our drinks and left quietly, seeking another safe haven.

Bob Honohan brokered a peace deal between myself and Billy before we boarded the plane the following day. I apologised. Forgiveness was not easily forthcoming. It took a bit of time. Eventually Billy let it go. Back home I had to write a letter of explanation and apology. Bob was the man for that. He even included a bit of Irish. Tadhg Murphy and himself had a competition to see who could write the best letter.

I got a report of the happenings at the next county board meeting when the issue was aired and my letter read out. Frank Murphy reportedly said that he had never come across anything like it before and I would have to be dealt with severely. He then recommended that I would be warned about my future conduct.

He was giving me a break. It wasn't the last time that Frank helped me out. He has a certain reputation in the GAA for being serious, an old-school type who wrote the rule book. But Frank is very loyal, a proud Corkman. We didn't always agree on everything but I always knew that if I needed support Frank would be there to provide it.

Back in the comfort of home I quickly put New York out of my mind. I had no desire to return.

•••••

The foyer of The Burlington Hotel is packed with revellers. All from Cork. As I step out of the lift I am struck by the wall of noise. Laughter and song. Cork are the All-Ireland senior football champions.

It is September 17, and I am the centre of attention. It's not a place where I am comfortable. I don't like attention. People say they think I'm shy. No, I just don't like it when there's a fuss about. My mother always preached the value of humility and I think that is what it is.

Today, I joined a very exclusive club.

The members are those who have won All-Ireland football medals in both hurling and football. There are so many famous names, legends of both games, that I certainly feel humbled to be included amongst them. Denis Walsh is on the list too. He didn't play today in the final but he has earned his medal.

As I step into the foyer people clap me on the back, shake hands. I meet friends. They embrace me. Some of the family are here. I have already chatted with them. Meeting up with them have been the best moments since the final whistle sounded.

I am privileged. All of the players are. Movement is not easy but space seems to open up for us. People stand back to let us through. We don't have to queue at the bar. Drinks seem to appear from nowhere.

You don't drink a lot on the night of a game. You're too tired, really. And there are duties to attend to. The official reception and interviews, especially with the television people. You don't want to go on live TV looking the worse for wear. You have also spent months living a very disciplined life and that is not abandoned easily.

Through the throngs I see a group of people, some of whom I know and a girl that I definitely don't know. A couple of the people call to me. I go over, shake hands and share a laugh.

"I'm Oonagh," she says.

"Teddy," I reply.

"I know."

Oonagh O'Neill from Passage, John and Thomas's sister. How has it taken so long to meet her? Were they hiding her from me? Keeping secrets from their old mate.

I want to spend time with her this evening, but it is not easy. So many people want to talk. They are excited. They have spent a lot of time and money supporting us and they deserve something back. But now, I would just like some time to spend with Oonagh, to get to know her a bit better. It's not possible, but I resolve there and then to make sure that it will happen soon.

It has been a long day.

A tough one.

There was tension going into this final. Having lost two we couldn't even contemplate losing a third. We were strong favourites to win it as well. That added to the tension. We knew Mayo would not roll over. They made it really hard, by far the hardest game of the year.

I was happy. I had played well in the final. It was my best year with Cork. John O'Neill, Oonagh's secretive brother and my great friend, had told me when he met me in America last May that he had never seen me as fit. I was like a gazelle, he said, a pure athlete.

I felt it too.

I was so healthy, so strong.

It was a good feeling.

It had been another busy summer. The hurlers drew with Waterford in the first round in Munster, 0-18 each. We were going through a lot of changes. I had another new partner at midfield, John Griffen from the 'Barrs. It had been Paul O'Conner from Na Piarsaigh the year before. Building a new team was taking time.

Two weeks later Paul and Jim Cashman were in midfield. I was centre-forward and scored one of our goals. Waterford beat us by two points.

The footballers didn't play me in the Munster semi-final. I was glad, for a change. My feet were sore. I had blisters. There was very little I could do except to stop playing. And I had no intention of doing that. Grounds were hard, I was training almost every day and playing every Sunday. I was on the sales team at Beamish & Crawford that summer. If I was working out near Kinsale I would head for Garretstown Beach and walk in the sea during lunchtime, letting the salt do its healing work. It certainly eased the pain but the blisters kept returning.

Cork beat Tipperary by sixteen points. I was a small bit worried that they might not pick me for the Munster final. The one game I did not want to miss was the Kerry game. Happily, the selectors kept faith in me.

A few weeks before the game, I heard that Kerry's young midfielder, Dermot Hanafin, had broken his leg. It was a bad blow for a guy with a lot of talent. I realised just how lucky I was. I might have been sore but it was nothing compared to Hanafin's pain.

We didn't play well in the final. Neither did Kerry. Maybe it was the heat of the day. Or maybe it was inevitable. The pendulum had swung. We were now the force. The great Kerry team had come to its natural end. We had beaten them comfortably in a League game just a few months previously. We knew they were not the force of old. We only won by three points but I don't think I was ever worried during that game that we would lose.

I think we were all relieved to hear the result of the Leinster final. Dublin had beaten Meath. We were sick of the sight of Meath by then. I wasn't afraid of them and I was convinced that we were good enough to beat them. But it was good to have a change. And Dublin would ensure a great atmosphere in Croke Park. We all looked forward to that.

That Cork team was at the height of its powers. We had a great panel and that was crucial. It didn't matter who played, who came on during a game, it never weakened the team. We were confident, believed in our ability. Just look at our bench in '89: Tony Nation had been a regular but, with Steven O'Brien breaking through and Mick Slocum playing so well, Tony was a sub. Denis Walsh was on the bench as well. Mick McCarthy and John O'Driscoll were brilliant footballers who were on and off the starting fifteen. Danny Culloty never played a poor game but it was very hard for him to hold on to a regular place because we had so many players.

Colm O'Neill was one of the best I played with. Michael Burns was another great talent and Eoin O'Mahony played some brilliant games for us. These were serious footballers. There was also great versatility amongst the players. Take Barry Coffey, for example. He played at wing-forward, wing-back and midfield that season. Jimmy Kerrigan had played wing-forward for us and, during 1989, alternated between half-back and corner-back.

With Colman missing because of his Achilles injury, Steven O'Brien moved to full-back. It was seamless. Tony Davis played right corner-back against Dublin and left half-back against Mayo in the All-Ireland final.

Myself, Shea, Larry, Barry and Danny could be selected at midfield. Shea was the only one who never moved. The others who were constant in their positions were Niall at corner-back, Conor at No.6, Paul McGrath at right corner-forward and John Cleary in the left corner. Dave Barry and Dinny Allen would switch around during games.

The Cork production line had worked well. Bob Honohan's work with the Under-21s was invaluable. And then Larry and Shea were added to the mix. We knew we had the ability to win an All-Ireland and I felt better in '89 than at any other time in my career.

The semi-final against Dublin was a strange game. They were 1-4 to 0-0 up after less than fifteen minutes. We weren't playing badly. They were just on fire. Then they conceded two penalties. Cleary slotted them both and we set sail.

Dublin's Keith Barr was sent off just before half time. I didn't see what happened. A lovely guy to meet, typical Dub with a great sense of humour and no airs and graces, he was a nuisance on the pitch. He was always at you. Talking and niggling, anything to get an advantage. Keith wasn't the only player who would do that sort of thing. It is part of the game. He just seemed to be more annoying than anyone else. He made a mistake that day. Dinny Allen wasn't taking any messing and, after one physical exchange, the referee noticed Keith out of the corner of his eye and gave him his marching orders.

The referee, the former Sligo star Mickey Kerins, wasn't happy with some of the stuff that went on during that half. I didn't think it was bad. Anyway, he called Dinny who was our captain and the Dublin captain, Gerry Hargan, together at the start of the second half just under the old Hogan Stand. I have never seen that happen before or since. They were told to speak to us and we were to behave. And I don't remember Dinny saying a word.

There were four points between us at the end, 2-10 to 1-9, and we were cruising. For the fourth consecutive year, I would play in an All-Ireland senior Championship final.

Since the season began the previous October, we had played fifteen competitive games. We won thirteen of them and drew one. The only team to beat us was Mayo. And who would we face in the final? You've guessed it. They could have beaten us again and that would have broken us. It was probably that fear that affected us in the final.

I was more nervous before that final than I could remember being before any game. Everyone was telling us that we were certain to win and every time I heard it the cagier I became. As often as people would remind us that we were hot favourites they would also add that we had lost the previous two finals and couldn't let it happen again.

Mayo were far better than everyone was saying. They were well coached by John O'Mahony who would prove his credentials as a team manager years later when leading Galway to All-Ireland success. Jimmy Burke played at full-forward for them in the final and he was taking us to the cleaners. When he got injured and had to go off just before half time we thought it might get easier. Then Anthony Finnerty came on and got a goal and missed another good chance.

It had been a hard slog for us. Mayo had big men around the middle of the field, none of them bigger than Liam McHale. They also had the Maher brothers, Sean and Greg, and the great Willie Joe Padden. His career was nearing its end but you could feel the class oozing out of him.

I had only experienced fear on the field once before, the day we were a point behind Galway in the '87 semi-final. We almost blew it that day. I felt fear again in the '89 final. We weren't messing up this time; we were being beaten by a team playing better than us. Was it fear that inspired me? I don't know. But early in the second half I knew I had to up my work-rate, fight for everything. I began to win ball in the air; if it broke I was onto it. I was passing fluently. The scores came. I got two points myself on the day. Mick McCarthy came on and scored two important points.

When the referee, Paddy Collins, blew the final whistle we had won by three points, 0-17 to 1-11. We were finally All-Ireland Champions. It felt great. I won an All Star award at midfield along with Willie Joe. It is my only All Star, although they did make a special presentation to me in 1990 to mark my 'double' victory.

And I was named as the Texaco Award winner for Gaelic football. That was a banquet I enjoyed because I met so many other sports people. Nicky English won the hurling award. Marcus O'Sullivan, another Cork man, was the athletics winner. Jockey Mick Kinane, golfer Ronan Rafferty, cyclist Sean Kelly, the boxer Dave 'Boy' McAuley, Ken Doherty the snooker champion, swimmer Gary O'Toole and soccer player Ronnie Whelan all won awards. That's good company.

Mick Higgins, the former Cavan footballer, won the Hall of Fame award. He told me that night, that he'd been born in New York. So, Danny isn't the only Yank to win an All-Ireland medal! I couldn't wait to tell him.

Before all that socialising I had other serious business to attend to. Sarsfields reached the Cork senior hurling Championship final for the first time since 1957. Joe McGrath had come on board as our coach at the start of the season and brought a new, professional, approach to our preparation. He was an inspirational figure who showed us what was needed to become the best. We faced Glen Rovers in the final. It was regarded as one of the best finals in Cork in many years. They won 4-15 to 3-13. It was disappointing, especially for some of our older players, like Bertie Og Murphy who had soldiered for so long and done so much to get us into a position to contest a final.

For the rest of us there was the knowledge that we had a young group of hurlers and we felt confident we would win one in the future. We didn't realise how long we would have to wait to get to another final. Eight more years.

I had a regular partner for the journeys to the awards ceremonies in Dublin during that winter of 1989 and 1990. I had succeeded in convincing Oonagh O'Neill to spend more time with me. I knew I had found my partner in life.

The O'Neills are a great sporting family. Hurling is part of their lives. Oonagh's mother, Phil, was an outstanding camogie player. John and Thomas were great teammates of mine. I felt at home in their home in Passage.

It was there, in August of 1990, that I watched the Cork football team win the All-Ireland semi-final without me. I was close to despair about my chances of recovery from my ankle injury. I thought my place in history would be snatched from me because of a weakness in my ankle ligaments. Oonagh, Phil and the lads provided comfort and support.

It wasn't easy for any of the Cork players to have a relationship because we were dedicated to our sport. I was involved in a game every weekend, either football or hurling. I might go out for a drink on a Saturday night but would be home early. I couldn't go on weekends away because I always had a game. That wasn't much fun for a partner.

Just one example of my commitments was the Easter weekend of April 16 and 17, 1990. I played for the footballers in the National League semi-final against Meath on Sunday and lined out for the hurlers the following day in their semi-final replay against Wexford. We lost both.

My old friend Mick Lyons wasn't having much sympathy for me. He battered me with one belt during the football game. He was booked, shrugged his shoulders and walked away. No talk, no complaint. I was lying on the ground seeing stars. That was the one game I do remember where there was obvious friction between the teams. Niall was sent off after a tussle with Colm O'Rourke. Others could have gone with him.

The hurling defeat hurt in a different way. Wexford won by 1-9 to 0-6 in Kilkenny's Nowlan Park. Six points scored in 70 minutes. We only scored two from frees in the second half. I will never forget reading Paddy Downey's report in *The Irish Times* the following day. His last line was a comment on our second-half display in front of goal.

"A pathetic return," he called it.

Paddy, a proud Corkman, was right.

I remember walking back from the ground to Langton's Hotel on John's Street in Kilkenny where a meal had been arranged. There were lads sobbing. Tears flowed freely. We were shocked by how we had played. All the positivity that followed the appointment the previous autumn of Fr O'Brien as our manager and Gerald McCarthy as coach had disappeared. We were in despair.

Five months later, thirteen of the fifteen who had started in Nowlan Park started the All-Ireland final. The transformation was remarkable. It was a tribute to the players that they could pick themselves up from the depths of despondency. It was also a tribute to the Padre and Gerald. They never lost faith. They didn't panic, just quietly worked away on confidence as well as teamwork.

We played Kerry on May 20 in the opening round of the hurling Championship. We didn't play well, but got through it. A week later I was out with the footballers against Limerick. We won 4-15 to 1-3. Seven days later we played Waterford in the Munster hurling semi-final. Just over 15,000 attended. Even our own faithful followers had doubts.

Cork 4-15, Waterford 1-8.

Back on course – and then I go for a ball in a nothing game up in Mayo, and end up in plaster.

From this remove, I wonder was rest the best thing that could have happened to me. I didn't feel fatigued at the time but I know I was training all the time and playing lots of games, many of them highly-charged Championship games. When I did resume playing in September I was fresh. I felt good.

It might not have made any difference at all. I'm not great with all this psychology anyway. I remember Billy bringing in a psychologist to talk to us one year before we played Kerry. I'm not knocking the science, but I just thought that if a Cork footballer needed a psychologist to help him prepare mentally to play Kerry then he shouldn't be playing at all.

I finished 1990 in a unique position in the history of the GAA as the only player to win All-Ireland medals in senior hurling and senior football in the same year. I became a father for the first time.

Oh, by the way, I didn't even get a nomination for either the hurling or football All Stars!

CHAPTER**11**

THE REBEL

I heard a quote some years ago, I think it was from Groucho Marx, who said, "I would not join a club that would have me as a member."

While I was delighted to accept membership of the dual All-Ireland winners club, I held sole membership of another exclusive club, early in 1991, that I would not have willingly applied for and would have happily given up.

We were in Canada for St Patrick's Day.

The Canadian GAA Board was celebrating an anniversary and a number of exhibition games were arranged for the SkyDome arena in Toronto. The stadium had been opened just two years earlier and was the only sports arena in North America with a retractable roof. It was built to host baseball and American football, but hosted many other events in an effort to pay the enormous cost of building the stadium, estimated at C$600million.

The Cork footballers and hurlers were invited to play the 1990 All Stars in the two-match programme. I was selected to play in both games. We were unsure about the effects of playing on an artificial surface and it was quietly agreed that if I was too tired after the football I would be replaced during the hurling game.

The problem didn't arise. What was supposed to be an exhibition became competitive. There were a couple of belts going around. I took a few. Paddy Russell, the referee, tried to get us to calm down. Eventually he had to do something.

Why did he pick on me?

I was sent off. I had picked one of the biggest men around to hit. Conor Deegan from Down. Right in front of Russell. What ammunition for the jokers: Teddy is the first footballer to be sent off on three continents – Europe, Australia and North America. I think I am the only member of that exclusive club.

Less than four months later, I would take another lonely walk.

•••••

The corridor beneath the stands at Semple Stadium are almost empty by the time I leave the dressing room. It is almost 6pm on the evening of July 7, 1991, and I am in a dilemma.

"What the hell am I going to do with myself for the rest of the summer?"

For the first time in eight years I would have no commitments to Cork hurling or football during the months of August and September. I had been involved in an All-Ireland final every year since 1983 when I played for the minor footballers in Croke Park.

In the last five Championships I had been involved in a senior final every year. I had played in a total of seven finals, five football including a replay, and two hurling.

I had started the 1991 season as an All-Ireland champion in both codes. And now there is nothing. A wilderness.

Then I spot Oonagh.

She has Cian in her arms.

My focus shifts.

Other members of her family are also waiting. Denis and a couple of his pals are with them. I know they are concerned for me, anxious about how I will react after a narrow defeat at the end of a very tense game. Tipperary has just mugged us in a replay. We should have retained the Munster title the first day in The Park – the lads scored three goals in the first half, Pat Fox got a late point to draw the game.

I had played as a sub that day. I had started the replay and played well.

Some daft stuff had gone on. There were two pitch invasions by Tipperary supporters celebrating two goals. It had been dangerous. Too many people had been let into the ground anyway.

Today, we had led by nine points in the second half and they still won the game. Crazy. They scored 2-5 in twenty minutes. This wouldn't have happened a year earlier.

I said after we lost to Kerry in the first round of the football Championship that we were a tired team. The football Championship wasn't seeded for the first time in decades. Fate decreed Cork and Kerry would meet first. We weren't ready.

This season the hurlers have not endured the same schedule but I still think there is an element of fatigue about the team. That's not an excuse. We were nine points ahead and that is not the sort of lead you should lose at any level. Already people are saying this was a classic Munster final. I don't care. We've lost.

There is another strange feeling about all of this. I am disappointed, but in some ways relieved. Such emotions should not equate.

Away from football and hurling I have been very busy. Oonagh and I were married in March. She is working very hard in a travel agency. I am doing promotions for Beamish & Crawford and that means lots of late nights. Like all parents with a newborn baby we are getting used to a changed lifestyle. Our nights are no longer our own. I am developing a greater appreciation for the commitment of some of the players I have soldiered with who have raised families while playing inter-county football and hurling.

For the first time since it all began, I am questioning the wisdom of trying to play two games at the highest level. It hasn't bothered me up to now but my life is changing. I have other responsibilities. It never bothered me before that I was committed to hurling and football six nights a week. The one night I had off, Saturday, was the night before a game. Now I am married and need to spend time with Oonagh. We have a baby boy to look after.

It is hard to think too much about the future so soon after a defeat. Hurling is my first choice but I would find it very difficult to walk away from the footballers after all the success we have enjoyed and all the fun we've had. I have good friends on the football team. We are still a relatively young outfit.

There hadn't been much talk of three in a row. Instead, all the attention had focussed on the All-Ireland double of 1990. It was historic and no one looked to the future. It was just as well. We were under no pressure before the football game with Kerry and there was no dramatic let-down when we were beaten.

I hated losing but that loss doesn't count amongst the worst. I feel more hurt about losing to Tipperary this year. It's a game we should have won. Can I continue to give my best to both teams? It is something I am going to have to think about before the end of the year.

I decide to put all those thoughts aside for a few months at least. Now that Cork are out of both Championships I can do some of the things I haven't been able to do since I became an adult. Weekends away.

A holiday?

I'd rather be playing.

•••••

There is a move to shaft Billy as our coach. No one explains why. He has been the most successful coach in Cork's football history. His team stumbled this year but we have won four Munster Championships and two All-Irelands. No one could possibly have expected more.

As a unit the players support him. We hear about reports of a breakdown in discipline. Someone has claimed at a county board meeting that on weekends away we are doing nothing but drinking. They don't know Billy if they think he allows that sort of stuff. He lets us have a few drinks from time to time. We have to relax. It can't be serious every hour and every minute. There has to be enjoyment, too.

But Billy is very professional in the way he prepares his teams. He has never put up with any messing. How would we have lasted through four very demanding years at the top of our game if he hadn't insisted on the highest standards?

It sounds to all of us as if someone is trying to shaft him. Billy doesn't bother with making himself popular, especially with administrators. This looks like payback time. The players voice their support for him. I think it helps.

Eventually he is reselected. He shouldn't have to prove himself any more. Knowing Billy, he will work even harder.

As the year approaches closure I have already lined out in the National Leagues with both teams. I got the call and I answered. I didn't make any decision. Neither the Padre nor Billy put any pressure on me. I got the notice and I turned up. I had given a couple of interviews in which I said I was considering my future. That created a small bit of a stir.

Some friends did question me.

I remained non-committal.

"Let's see what happens," is my attitude.

It was no big deal in the end. I just got on with it. Doubts disappeared. I stayed a dual player. I would be around until they decided to get rid of me. That's the way it should be.

•••••

It is May, 1992.

Four days to go to another Championship clash with Kerry and I am lying on a trolley in the Regional Hospital in Cork city. I now know what a blinding headache is. My eyes are tightly shut and I am still in pain, bright lights seem to be piercing my eyelids.

Normally, I would be relishing the prospect of a crack at Kerry, particularly after they broke our winning streak a year ago. But I am actually afraid. I know there is something wrong. I'm moaning, I'm a lousy patient.

"Where's the doctor?" I ask Oonagh a hundred times.

I hadn't been feeling well at the start of the week but put it down to the fact that I had been working long hours. Beamish & Crawford had hosted a vintners' weekend in the city. There were two days of golf out in Little Island and a conference at the new centre attached to the Silver Springs Hotel.

The hotel was one of my calls so I was running myself ragged to ensure that everything went right. I certainly had to ensure that the supply of all our products was plentiful, that all the signage was correct and in position. I was putting on a show. All the company bosses were attending and I was determined that everything would go like clockwork.

I had trained on Tuesday evening. Feeling lousy, I spoke to Billy. He sent me home and told me to rest. Oonagh sent me straight to bed. I couldn't sleep. The room was completely dark but I felt like I was lying under floodlights. The pain gradually got worse and worse. In the morning Oonagh drove me to hospital.

Three hours later I am still waiting to be seen and I am getting a bit frantic. I think my head is going to explode. Oonagh rings Dr Con. I do not know what he does but, soon afterwards, a doctor arrives at my trolley and orders that I be transferred to a bed.

He mentions something that I later learn is a procedure called a lumbar puncture. I don't know what that is but I just want him to do it so that I will be free of pain. Then I see the needle. It is huge. I'm asked to bend over on the edge of the bed. Pain shoots through me. I fall.

They get me back in bed and perform the lumbar puncture. Then they give me medication. I sleep for a long time, and when I wake I ask Oonagh what is wrong with me.

Viral meningitis.

"It's only a mild form," she soothes me, as she sees fear flame in my eyes. "You'll be fine. The doctor says just to rest."

"But, the match on Sunday?"

"You can't be even thinking of that," she says.

It is the following morning, Thursday, and all the pain is gone. Billy calls in and asks how I am. "Great, it was just a virus. I'll be fine for Sunday."

He goes away happy.

Just a virus!

The doctor tells me I can go home on Friday. Complete rest for a few days.

"But I'm playing against Kerry on Sunday," I blurt.

The doctor and Oonagh tell me I'm crazy. Maybe I am, but I'm not missing a game against Kerry. I sign a form saying something about playing against medical advice. I don't know if it is indemnifying the hospital and the doctors. I'll sign anything in order to play.

At home I sleep for hours on Friday and then right through the night. I haven't felt as good in a year or two. The rest has rejuvenated me. I meet with the team on Saturday evening. Just for a chat. Someone hears I had viral meningitis.

"Doesn't you brain swell with that?" someone says.

"Should you be playing at all?" someone else asks.

"No problem there," says another, Mick McCarthy probably.

"Sure we all know … he doesn't have a brain."

The following day I'm wearing No.9 but playing at centre half-forward. Larry has an infection in a leg. Shea and Danny are in midfield. Danny has been struggling with an injury but starts. Barry is another coming off the casualty list. Ambrose O'Donovan and Noel O'Mahony from Tralee are 8 and 9 for Kerry.

I am flying. Maurice Fitzgerald gives them an advantage when he scores a first-half penalty. I pick up a loose ball to the right of the Kerry goal and hit a good dipping shot. It clips the crossbar and goes over. It was a chance.

We kick just two wides in the second half, but both are from penalties. Niall Cahalane, who scored a point earlier, misses the first penalty. Shea misses the second. A corner-back and a midfielder taking penalties?

The world is gone mad, I think.

I'm the only one of the six starting forwards who scores from play and I do that when I have moved out to midfield. Joe Kavanagh kicks five points from frees. It's a pity he hadn't taken the penalties! He's a newcomer but place-kicking is one of his strengths.

Kerry win by 2-14 to 0-10. Billy O'Shea got their second goal with virtually the last kick of the game. It's a ten-point defeat but it doesn't feel like it. It seems much closer than that. I have probably played my best game against Kerry and we've lost.

Two years in a row we've been beaten by them. It hurts. Little do I know how much that hurt will intensify when they are shocked by Clare in the Munster final. Okay, it is great for Clare to get such an unexpected reward. But if we had beaten Kerry I don't think we would have lost to Clare.

At the end of September, Donegal win their first All-Ireland title. Is that one that got away? No disrespect to Donegal or Clare, but I think if we had accounted for Kerry we would have been too strong for everyone else that summer. We'll never know, of course, but I think we should have won our third title in 1992.

•••••

I'm on strike.

It's the middle of November and I am at war with the Cork football selectors. They've dropped me because I played a club game on the day of a National League game, so I've told them I am not playing any more.

It's a one-man protest that some of the lads have tried to talk me out of. But the club comes first with me and I want an apology.

We were due to play Carlow in the National Football League in Pairc Ui Chaoimh. Division Two football isn't the glamorous stuff we are accustomed to but we have been taking it seriously. We need to get back into the top division and picking up two points against the likes of Carlow is important.

On the morning of the game, November 15, I had walked down to the local pitch. The Glanmire intermediate footballers were playing a League game at 11am. Normally I would have been playing but I was due at Jury's Hotel at midday to meet with the county footballers.

The players were arriving slowly. By the time the match had started Glanmire had only fourteen players. I told the selectors not to worry, some guy would drag himself out of bed in time for the second half. There's a regulation that a team must start the second half with fifteen players, or else they forfeit the points.

At half time no one had arrived. I decided to run up to the house and get my gear. The Glanmire kit bag with the right gear was, as usual, already packed with neatly ironed and folded togs and socks. I brought the Cork bag as well because I knew I would be rushing away later. Once the club game ended I rang the hotel and explained to one of the selectors what had happened and that I would be late. There was no point in making up a story. They would find out when the referee's report was handed in later in the week anyway.

Sitting beside Conor Counihan in the dressing room in the ground I could see the selectors in a huddle. It wasn't a guess as to what they were discussing.

Me.

I turned to Conor.

"If those guys drop me today you won't see me around here again."

"Cool it, don't do anything rash that you might regret later," he advised.

The chairman of the selectors, Martin Crowley, walked over. He told me he was sorry, that he had bad news. Because I had played for the club in the morning the selectors felt I wouldn't be able to give my best.

"I'll be the judge of that," I told him. "I feel well able to give my best. If I don't do it on the pitch then you guys can make a judgement. Take me off then if you want."

They wouldn't be convinced.

I was dropped.

So, I took off my gear and put on my clothes. As I walked towards the door I got a tap on the shoulder.

Billy.

"Where are you going?"

"Fuck you and fuck Cork!" I roar. "My club comes first ... same as Nemo is first for you."

I was gesticulating with my hands when I said this. I was mad. I pushed Billy in the chest to emphasise my point. He slipped on the tiles. I walked away and didn't look back. I left the ground.

Since then, phone calls have been made.

Billy has spoken to me.

I am looking for an apology.

The club has lodged a letter of protest with the county board. I play with the hurlers the following Sunday. Some of the lads ask me if I will be back with the footballers the following week.

Not unless I get an apology, I say.

The footballers train in Delaney's GAA Club on the old Mallow road where Billy asks me to meet him. I am still looking for an apology but I don't get it. Billy and I thrash it out. He asks me to forget about it. He wants me to play for Cork.

I say ok.

Strike over.

Teddy the Rebel.

CHAPTER**12**

DUAL DUELS

The dual player has always enjoyed a special status in the eyes of the GAA supporter. It has certainly had a huge impact on my life. I am proud, if a little humbled, to be fêted in this role along with so many legends of the game.

Often during my life, however, I have had occasion to wonder if the people who run the GAA actually appreciate the valuable asset that they have in the dual player. I don't believe they do. In fact, I believe they would be happier if there was no such thing.

Let me first relate a positive story.

It has been sixteen years since I played for Cork. I haven't had a very high profile in that time, only occasionally straying into the limelight, and sometimes for the wrong reasons. But I am still privileged to be recognised, and to have nice things said to me and about me.

Earlier this year, around February, I was having a drink on a Saturday night in Glanmire with some friends. The bar was fairly full when a girl in her 20s approached me.

"Are you Teddy McCarthy?" she asked.

I'm not always comfortable in these situations. The lads often give me a good bit of slagging about being a celebrity. On this night they were polite.

When I confirmed I was Teddy she explained her approach. She was from Cavan and visiting a friend from Glanmire with whom she had qualified as a nurse. Earlier that week, she had told her father where she would be spending the weekend.

"If you're going to Glanmire," he told her earnestly, "then make sure you meet Teddy McCarthy."

We had a good chat and I have to admit that I do enjoy the fact that a man way up in Cavan still remembers me and thinks it important that his daughter should meet me. Supporters like that are the lifeblood of the GAA and if the dual player feeds their passion and their dreams then I would think the GAA should encourage dual participation. More often than not, however, it actually discourages the dual role.

Sometimes a clash is unavoidable. I had a very early experience of that. It was early February of 1985. I had been training with the hurlers that winter and actually played a challenge game against Waterford during January of '85. The National hurling and football Leagues were due to resume on the first Sunday in February. I expected to be playing with the footballers against Armagh and was duly named to line out against the likes of Joe Kernan.

I was surprised, even amazed, when I heard that I had also been selected to play for the hurlers for the very first time, in their game against Galway.

What made it even more complicated was that adverse weather conditions meant Pairc Ui Chaoimh could not host both games. Midleton was chosen as the venue for the hurling game. Whatever chance I had at 19 years of age of playing the two games in the one venue, I did not have the knack of bi-location.

Fortunately, the decision was taken by others. Representatives of the two selection committees met and it was agreed that the needs of the footballers that weekend were greater than the hurlers'. Clashes were, thankfully, infrequent and I always left it to the team managements to decide what I should do.

Years later, however, I found myself in the crazy position in 1992 of having to choose between the hurlers and the footballers for the first round of the Munster Championship. Despite the fact that Cork has the record for producing more dual inter-county players than any other county, the Munster Council fixed the Cork hurlers and footballers to open their Championship campaigns on the same day, May 24.

I had indicated a couple of times, after 1990, that I would end my dual commitment because the demands were becoming too great. But the managers were considerate and encouraging. The training was a burden but I was enjoying the games and when I was free of injury I was feeling really good and strong.

Situations like this made me question the wisdom of going on. Why was I putting myself through all of this when people were placing ridiculous barriers in front of me? I could understand this happening in the Leagues. But there was no reason whatsoever for having this kind of clash in the Championship.

At least they did decide that the two teams would play at the same venue – Pairc Ui Chaoimh.

Kerry provided the opposition in both codes. Was that the reason the fixtures-makers decided on a double-header? Did they assume the Kerry hurlers would be cannon-fodder for Cork and decide it would be a handy way to get a meddlesome fixture out of the way? They probably thought that the Cork hurling management would not be too worried about my potential absence and that I would be happy to stick with the footballers for what would be considered a more demanding test. But that is not the way players or their coaches think.

Maybe I'm being presumptuous.

They probably didn't consider the dual player issue at all.

The Padre and Gerald had been working hard with the hurlers all through the winter. They had tried different formations. I had played a couple of games in the League in the half-back line. They were trying things out to build a team to challenge for the Championship.

A few new guys were making a mark. Brian Corcoran was already creating quite a stir as the most promising young player in the country. Cathal Casey and David Quirke were also challenging for places. Barry Egan and Ger Manley were in the panel. Competition was hotting up.

When the Championship came along I wasn't available for the first round. It was an unnecessary inconvenience. It could easily have cost me my place on the hurling team. It didn't happen but they weren't to know that when making the fixture.

It didn't cause a problem for me in choosing who to train with and play for because Billy and Fr O'Brien had a good relationship and would work these things out. They would then speak to me and my schedule would be finalised. But I thought it was unfair. It didn't show respect to Kerry, to Cork, to the managers, to me or to the concept of the dual player.

I played with the footballers.

We lost.

The hurlers won.

Two weeks later, the hurlers played Tipperary in the Munster semi-final. Who featured on the front cover of the match programme? You've guessed it. The guy who'd had to choose football over hurling two weeks earlier! It's very hard to make sense out of that.

It was a huge game, a meeting of the 1990 and 1991 All-Ireland champions. There had been a number of cracking games between the counties since Tipperary had re-emerged as a major force in the late 1980s. Our team that had won the 1990 hurling All-Ireland was still fairly intact. Denis Mulcahy missed the following season but returned for 1992 and added experience. Ger Fitzgerald was captain for '92 and that was a motivation for us to do well. Corcoran was only eighteen years old but made himself a permanent fixture in the Championship. Timmy Kelleher was another to come through the supply line. Sean McCarthy from Ballinhassig was my partner at midfield.

Corcoran restricted Pat Fox to just two points. Nicky English was marked by Sean O'Gorman and didn't score. We won by a goal, 2-12 to 1-12. The North Mon lads, Tony and Tomas, got the goals. Still going strong. It was another tight affair. We never had anything else against Tipperary and it was good to get it out of the way.

A couple of weeks later I played for Sarsfields in the Cork senior Championship. I was suffering real discomfort with my right knee. I was hobbling. It wasn't anything like a ligament injury but it was persistent and sore. It was my first dose of cartilage trouble.

It was obvious that I would have to have surgery on the knee, and the sooner the better. Initially, I was ruled out of the Munster final. I wasn't completely immobile and thought that I could play some part against Limerick. I talked to Fr O'Brien. It was agreed I would be named in the subs. Surgery was delayed until after the game. I surprised everyone when I came on as a sub in a five-point win for us. We were Munster champions again and we hadn't been out of Pairc Ui Chaoimh all summer, and now we were going back to familiar territory.

Croke Park.

It wasn't my favourite ground to play on but I had missed it.

The following week I had an appointment in Tralee General where the surgeon, Fionan Carroll, did the corrective work. I was a sub again for the All-Ireland semi-final. It was one of the rare occasions we played Down during that period. We won by 2-17 to 1-11. We would play Kilkenny, the beaten finalists of the previous year, in the All-Ireland final.

As I have already written, I didn't really like the Croke Park surface but I always enjoyed the experience of being involved in a final. And this would be the first time I would play against Kilkenny in the Championship. This clash of the traditional giants of hurling – we were going for Cork's 28th title and they were looking for Kilkenny's 24th – generated enormous interest everywhere.

It is strange to record now that, over the ten years I played senior hurling for Cork, I only played against Kilkenny once in the Championship. When you think of the great rivalry that has existed between us throughout the history of the GAA it seems extraordinary that that should be the case. It is a reflection of that era. The great rivalries were Cork and Tipperary, Tipperary and Galway, Offaly and Kilkenny. It was an exciting time to be involved because of the strength of Galway and Tipperary. Limerick began to make an impression towards the end of my career, and Wexford won an All-Ireland title as my career wound down. That was all good for hurling.

I remember that final day against Kilkenny as dark and dreary. It was reflective of both the elements and the result. A light rain fell in the morning as we made our way up to UCD for a puck-around. During the build-up, amidst the usual hype, ticket gathering and media duties, there had been a slight strain in the camp. Fr O'Brien and Gerald had decided to attempt some tactical switches that weren't going down well with some of the players.

Kevin Hennessy had been playing at full-forward, with John Fitzgibbon in one corner and Ger Fitz in the other. The management wanted Fitzgibbon to go full-forward with Kevin in the corner. The plan was that when an attack started, Kevin would move out to the half-forward line and the ball would be driven into the space for Fitzgibbon to run onto.

Kevin wasn't happy.

Neither was John.

He was blunt in his assessment.

"Father, you don't score goals from the corner flag," he argued.

We thought the idea had been ditched but, on the morning of the final, when we gathered in UCD, it was announced that Kevin would start in the corner and John at full-forward.

The two players were obviously taken aback. They didn't like the notion and their low mood spread through the team. We didn't feel comfortable going into the game, and, against a team as talented as Kilkenny were at the time, that was not good.

They had some really fine hurlers. The forward line that started was Liam McCarthy, John Power, DJ Carey, Eamon Morrissey, Liam Fennelly and Jamesie Brennan. The two subs that came on were Christy Heffernan and Adrian Ronan. That's some firepower.

They had decent players elsewhere. I was marked by Willie O'Connor until I moved to midfield. His brother, Eddie, was at corner-back. Pat Dwyer was full-back, Liam Simpson, Liam Walsh and Pat O'Neill were the other backs. Michael Walsh was in goal, and Mike Phelan and Bill Hennessy were in midfield.

Despite that strength we were in front at half time, 0-7 to 1-2. That scoreline reflects the conditions. It rained before the game and there was a wind behind us for the first half. Carey scored their 1-2, the goal from a penalty.

We also hit seven wides in that half and they would prove very costly. There was confusion through the team because of the positional changes. The tactic hadn't worked in training and had been discarded. It wasn't working now. As a team we didn't play well. I didn't play well, though I did get some favourable mentions in match reports the following day.

Early in the second half, John Power kicked a goal and kick-started their comeback. We could have won it but I'm not sure that we would have deserved it.

•••••

Only a few counties produce dual players at inter-county level. That is partly to do with size; partly with tradition. I fear for the future of the dual player. I hope I'm wrong but all the signs are that he is an endangered species.

I don't believe the authorities have wanted dual players for a long time because it is an inconvenience to their schedules. Actually, the dual player is a thorn in their side.

When they introduced the back door system to the Championship they sounded the death knell for the dual player. And now that the back door system applies at club level, I predict that the dual player will be extinct in our lifetime.

I know that I would not have lasted as long as I did had there been a qualifier system in the Championship when I played. I wonder would I have got the opportunity to win my unique place in the history of the GAA? By 1990, I would have had a lot of mileage completed. I was suffering injuries with the schedule I had. Imagine the demands if there had been qualifiers to contend with. It would have been impossible.

I fear for the dual player and that is a crying shame. Everyone who loves Gaelic Games loves to see the best players playing and that is not possible any more. More and more they are being forced to make choices because they simply cannot fit in all the games.

Forget about my own career and 1990.

Wouldn't it have been a terrible pity if the public had not been able to see Jimmy Barry Murphy and Ray Cummins playing football? I was only a kid when Jimmy played in 1973, but he inspired another generation with the way he played the game.

Liam Currams was an amazing athlete to win a hurling All-Ireland in 1981 and a football title the following year, with Offaly.

We seem to be forever trying to increase the number of games our players are playing. It is at an almost unsustainable level now for players sticking to one code only. It is impossible for a player to try and combine the two.

When I was growing up, and I know it is the same for my own two lads to this day, it was the natural thing to play hurling and football. In a county like Cork, one goes with the other. It is the same all over the country. I've just finished managing Laois and nearly all the players there play football as well as hurling. They don't do it at county level.

It's the same in places like Tipperary and Galway. Declan Browne played both football and hurling for Tipperary. He is unusual in that, when making a choice between the two, he chose football. Brendan Cummins, their outstanding goalkeeper, made the more orthodox choice but I know he is a very good footballer.

Alan Kerins won an All-Ireland football medal with Galway but was unlucky that the hurlers were beaten in the finals of 2001 and 2005. Kerins' involvement in those finals created a stir. It was something different and it inspired young lads in Galway and elsewhere.

I know there are dual players in Carlow and counties like Derry and Down. George O'Connor from Wexford was as good a footballer as he was a hurler.

Keith Higgins played in an All-Ireland football final for Mayo this year and I'm told he is a brilliant hurler and has tried to play as often as he can for Mayo. But it is getting too hard. I see there are a good few dual players in the successful Dublin minor teams of recent years. I expect they will face a choice very soon.

The list of dual players from the past is endless. I wonder will there be a list in the future at all. In Cork now, the only player who straddles both games at inter-county level is Eoin Cadogan. I wouldn't be sure there will be too many more in the future.

In the desire to create more and more games for our players at every level a terrible sacrifice is being made – the dual player is that sacrifice. I do not believe that it is good for the GAA.

For the record, the players to have won All-Ireland senior hurling and football Championship medals are:

WJ Spain (Tipperary) hurling 1889, football (Limerick) 1887

Bill Mackessy (Cork) hurling 1903, football 1911

Pierce Grace (Kilkenny) hurling 1911, 1912, 1913, football (Dublin) 1908

Sean O'Kennedy (Wexford) hurling 1910, football 1915, 1916, 1917

Paddy Mackey (Wexford) hurling 1910, football 1915, 1916, 1917, 1918

Frank Burke (a native of Kildare) hurling (Dublin) 1917, 1920, football (Dublin) 1921, 1922, 1923

Leonard McGrath (Galway) hurling 1923, football 1925

Jack Lynch (Cork) hurling 1941, 1942, 1943, 1944, 1946, football 1945

Paddy Healy (Cork) hurling 1944, 1946, football (sub) 1945

Derry Beckett (Cork) hurling 1942, football 1945

Ray Cummins (Cork) hurling 1970, 1976, 1977, 1978, football 1973

Denis Coughlan (Cork) hurling 1970 (sub), 1976, 1977, 1978; football 1973

Brian Murphy (Cork) hurling: 1976, 1977, 1978, football 1973

Jimmy Barry Murphy (Cork) hurling 1976, 1977, 1978, 1984, 1986, football 1973

Teddy O'Brien (Cork) hurling 1976 (sub), football 1973

Liam Currams (Offaly) hurling 1981, football 1982

Denis Walsh (Cork) hurling 1986, 1990, football (sub) 1989, (sub) 1990

And myself, Teddy McCarthy (Cork) hurling 1986, 1990, football 1989, 1990.

CHAPTER**13**

SIGN LANGUAGE

'Kid' looks at me incredulously.

Billy is in another corner of the dressing room with Steven O'Brien, Shea and two of the young lads, Colin Corkery and Joe Kavanagh. The Nemo gang together as usual. Billy's index finger is raised to a position at the side of his forehead and doing a circular motion.

"Mad," he mouths.

"Yer man is as mad as a hatter."

They're all laughing at my expense.

I remain indignant.

"I'm telling you, Kid, I had chicken pox when I was a boy. And I've just had them again," I insist, pointing to some of the fading spots on my upper body.

"Teddy, you can't get chicken pox twice. You might be a freak of nature but not even you can defy science," says Kid Cronin; masseur, kit man, chicken pox expert.

"Well, you better speak to the mother because she swears I had it before."

That prompted a round of guffaws from the bright sparks. I should have kept my mouth shut. Three weeks earlier, at the beginning of June, 1993, Oonagh and I had been passing through Rochestown – Cian was being cared for by

Oonagh's mother in Passage. He had chicken pox and we were relieved that baby Niall had not been affected. Niall had been born the previous October.

We'd spotted Jim Cashman and stopped for a chat. Jim and I had seen a lot of each other recently. Cork and Wexford played three times during the month of May, including two periods of extra time, before a winner of the National Hurling League final could be decided. We won. I had played in the first round of the football Championship the previous Sunday against Clare. The game had gone well. We had some new guys and they looked up to the mark.

I had the driver's side window down and was leaning slightly to my right to speak to Jim. Oonagh looked across and spotted the red blotch on my skin. Niall might have escaped, but I hadn't.

Jesus, I never knew you could be so sick with chicken pox. I was laid low for two weeks. My mother was mystified. She insisted that I'd had them as a young child. She went through all of her eight children and ticked off each one who'd had chicken pox. "Teddy, yes definitely," she would say, without a hint of doubt in her voice.

It was just one of the many dramas throughout the year that would mark the beginning of the end of my time with the Cork football and hurling teams.

●●●●●

I never thought much about taking a break during my years with Cork. Team managers would be accommodating. I was giving a lot, both physically and mentally, and they would have understood if I wasn't always available during the National Leagues. But when the competition began in October, often uncomfortably close to the conclusion of the Championship, and the opportunity to play arose with either team I generally made myself available. There was no great mystery to it. I enjoyed it. That was my life. I enjoyed playing and I enjoyed the company of the people I was playing with.

We had a good lifestyle. I would go so far as to suggest we were pampered and we enjoyed it. Travelling around Ireland on wintry Sundays might not sound like much fun, especially after a hard year of Championship action, but it was better than sitting at home doing nothing.

As the kids came along I did begin to think about being at home a bit more. Over the winter of 1992 and 1993, I began to notice a few changes in both dressing rooms. Some familiar faces were missing and there were more fresh-faced young fellas than usual. That was an incentive in its own way. It was a challenge. I liked to prove I was still good enough. I was well used to playing in All-Ireland finals at that stage of my career, but I had only once played in a League final, the football decider in 1989. I'm not sure what that says about the League. We didn't go out consciously not to reach finals or win them but, generally, we used the competition as preparation for the Championship.

Looking back on old files now I notice that we played a lot of football in Division Two of the League. It didn't do us any harm. It would have been a whole lot different in hurling, of course, but still we contested the final only once in the ten seasons that I lined out in the competition.

In the course of the League in 1992-93, we had played Wexford in Pairc Ui Chaoimh. We noted they were far more fired up than we were. They won by six or seven points and it was a big thing for them. They had watched us win All-Irelands and play in the final of 1992 so they were measuring themselves against us. Two months later we met again in the final. A little over 20,000 spectators attended the game. Nearly all of them were from Wexford and they made a lot of noise. They should have been celebrating at the end, too. John O'Connor, who took their long-range frees, had a chance to win the game with the last puck from a free but the ball went wide.

A week later we played extra time. Again, Wexford should have won it. Jim Cashman got a long-range point for us to equalise. Another replay was necessary, this time on the following Saturday. Thankfully, we put an end to it then on a 3-11 to 1-12 scoreline. I remember talking to some of the Wexford players afterwards. They were really disappointed. And they couldn't understand how blasé we were. Some of the lads hadn't waited on the pitch for the trophy presentation. That wasn't being arrogant or anything. We had a Championship game in two weeks and that was the priority. There wasn't time to celebrate.

Years later, one of the Wexford players told me that he had learned a lot from us during that series of games and it helped him when they went on to win an All-Ireland title in 1996. There was a reception held by the sponsors on the evening of the first Wexford game at a hotel in Thurles. The Padre, now Canon O'Brien, had us on a tight leash. It was soft drinks all round. But the Wexford lads availed of the plentiful supply of wine courtesy of the sponsors and, when the meal was over, they headed for the bar. We headed home.

I couldn't have celebrated after we eventually won the title. The footballers were to play Clare the following weekend in the first round of the Championship. Clare were Munster champions. They had stunned Kerry with a remarkable victory in 1992 and did themselves justice in the All-Ireland semi-final against Dublin.

Ours was a changing team. Lads like Mark Farr, Mark O'Connor, Ciaran O'Sullivan, Brian O'Donovan, Anthony Davis's brother, Don, and the new sensation from Nemo, Colin Corkery, were getting their chance. Corkery had spent some time trialling in Australian Rules but had come home. He scored 2-5 in his Championship debut that Sunday.

A couple of days later Oonagh spotted the spot.

•••••

Billy's finger is in the air again.

It's not circling now.

It is making a directional sign, first straight up, then the joints bending towards him. He repeats it a few times.

We call it "getting the finger".

It is not even half time in the All-Ireland football final and, for the first time in my inter-county career, I am being withdrawn from a game without an injury. I walk briskly from the pitch to the dug-out below the old Cusack Stand. I don't look at anybody.

I stare blankly.

One shitty way for this year to end, I think to myself.

Croke Park is rocking. Underneath dark grey skies there's a fierce battle going on out there. Joe Kavanagh has scored a brilliant goal for us. I had a hand in it. At least one pass from me that day had reached its intended target.

Don Davis got it.

Gave it to Joe.

He left three Derry backs in his wake.

Great finish.

Unfortunately, nearly everything else I had put my hand to seemed to find a Derry player.

Derry had qualified for an All-Ireland senior final for the first time since the 1950s. They had beaten Dublin with a late point in the semi-final. Their supporters are exuberant. Our supporters are making a fair bit of noise, too. The red and white flags, colours of both counties, seem to form a banner across the terraces at both ends of the field. The action is driving them into a frenzy.

There are big men on both sides. The challenges are physical. Shea and I are being clattered by Anthony Tohill and Brian McGilligan, my old friend from the Australia tour seven years ago. There's no malice. It's good, hard football.

There are a few malicious clatters being thrown elsewhere. I notice the Derry manager, a fiery lad named Eamonn Coleman, running onto the pitch to protest about something into the ear of the referee, Tommy Howard. If Meath's Gerry McEntee was out here Coleman might get a telling off. We ignore him.

Enda Gormley is stretched.

Niall Cahalane gets a warning from the referee.

He tells me later that he was lucky.

I'm not so lucky. Niall gets a ball in the corner. He moves out. I'm on my own. He fists it to me, at head height. I put up both hands but the ball slips through. McGilligan is behind me, he picks it up, and kicks it over the bar.

I give chase to Damien Cassidy. Might have got to him, too, except Niall and Stevo are coming from the other direction. I leave him to them. Cassidy fires the ball high to the right of our goal. I follow the flight, then look down. Mark O'Connor is standing on the edge of the square.

Kerinsy is on his line. Derry's full-forward, Seamus Downey, is on the move. I shout a word of warning. The boys can't hear it above the noise of the crowd. Downey gets his fist to the ball.

Goal.

Cahalane gets his hands on a breaking ball. Three Derry players surround him. He is targeted. Gets a puck in the mouth. Stays down. The ref gives us a free. I spot Barry Coffey and take the free quickly. As I strike the ball, Barry turns and sprints off unaware of my intentions. Fergal McCusker scoops up the ball and passes to Gormley. From under the Hogan Stand he sends the ball curling over the bar. Running back onto the field he passes Niall and shakes a couple of fingers at him.

The punch he got woke him up. He scored three quick points after that. Niall should have left him bloody well alone. Next ball I get, I see Shea. I could pass with the hand or the foot. I go with the foot. A Derry player intercepts.

Billy's finger tells me what to do next.

It's not easy watching from the old dug-out. It is sunk into the ground. Your head is just above ground. The bumps in the old pitch partially restrict your view. Danny Culloty has come on for me. He's a good guy. Danny only came home from America when he was 10 or 11. He played basketball and in training he often used some of his best techniques against me. If you were jumping for a ball with him he had a canny knack of hitting you with his hip and knocking you off balance. Great ploy. He is a natural, but had to work hard on his kicking. It has been some achievement for him to reach this level and stay at it.

There's a small bit of niggle in the game. Something happens on the far side of the field. I can't see it. The referee calls Tony Davis over.

Can't be much in that, I think. Davis is one of the cleanest footballers of all time.

Then Tommy Howard points to the line.

He is sending him off.

Incredible.

I only learned later how incredible. It was a terrible decision. Dermot Heaney went for a ball. He was crouching when Davis went in with his shoulder. It was a free, nothing more. Tony pays the price for the misdemeanours of others. The referee could not have made a poorer choice. My old theory about 14 men responding to a sending off is put to the test.

It is not a test we pass.

John O'Driscoll gets a great goal for us in the second half. We've put away two of the best goals I've ever seen scored by Cork but we're losing the game. I am really shattered to be sitting in the horrible dug-out looking on. At any other time of the year you know you are going to get a chance to redeem yourself. You think about the next game. Or you think about training and the next practise game, and you are already determined to prove your worth.

But this is the final.

There won't be another chance for me this year.

I notice Dermot McNicholl coming on. What a great footballer. He went to Australia for a while. His career was slowed by injuries but he retained his class. Derry win the title for the first time. The celebrations are wild. Good for them. I am glad for the likes of McNicholl, McGilligan and Tony Scullion who were with us in Australia. They're great men. It's a glorious time for Ulster football. I think about all of that later, though. Right now, I'm just thinking about everything I've been through this year.

I hadn't been fit enough after my bout of chicken pox to play in the Munster hurling semi-final against Clare. I went to the game as part of the squad. We lost by three points. It was a surprise and the end of an era. Canon O'Brien and Gerald were not reappointed.

The following Sunday I made one of my favourite journeys west of Cork city, to Killarney. The open draw in the Munster football Championship had, once again, paired the two great rivals in a semi-final. Jacko and Ambrose were gone. Only the Bomber remained from the golden years. Maurice Fitz and young Seamus Moynihan were the new stars. Kerry were still producing great footballers. It's a production line.

Dermot Hanafin was back after his leg break. Bernard McElligott was alongside him. Noel O'Mahony came on during the game. I was with Shea. We won by three points. Mick McCarthy scored 1-2. He was captain that year and you could feel his desire. I had been spring-heeled, caught a few big ones. The crowd had loved it. The Cork crowd, anyway.

In fairness, over the years some Kerry people have been most complimentary to me and supportive of me. Dr Jim Brosnan, a very popular man who won All-Irelands with Kerry in the 1950s, often praised me for my fielding. Paidi O Se was another who gave me a lot of credit.

After helping to beat Tipperary in the Munster football final I concentrated on the club. We were on a high after beating Aghada in a replay in the Cork senior Championship. My brother Denis was playing in goal and we were enjoying a good run. Glanmire played Skibbereen in Inishannon. I went for a big one. I got a bump in the air and came down on my left knee. It inflated like a balloon.

Fionan Carroll was on holidays. Dr Con made a phone call. Ray Moran was an orthopaedic surgeon in Dublin and his brother is Kevin, who played soccer for Manchester United and Ireland. He had a slot. There was a lot of damage so he had to remove something like 50 per cent of the cartilage. There was no chance I would make the semi-final. That was becoming something of a habit. Not a good one.

I had really been looking forward to playing Mayo. Jacko had taken over as their manager at the start of the season. It was a tough one for his first job. He took over when the county was in a lot of bother with plenty of in-fighting. The players had revolted against the previous manager who'd had them pushing cars around carparks as part of their training regime. Billy threatened us with the same.

He was joking.

We weren't sure.

Jacko won a Connacht title. It was a good start for him.

The lads ripped Mayo apart. Kavanagh, Coffey, Corkery, O'Driscoll and Mick Mc all scored goals. It was 5-15 to 0-10 in the end. Obviously, I hadn't been missed.

I'd never felt before that a lay off might affect my form. In fact, my belief had strengthened over the years that a rest was a good thing. To this day, I wonder could you give a team a week off training before an All-Ireland final or any other major game. Would it make them fresher? They say rest is an important part of any training programme. That would certainly put it to the test. I would love to try it. If it worked I'd be a genius. If it didn't? Well, you know.

I was selected for the final. I felt really good. John O'Neill was a shrewd observer. He told me that, while I was on the field in the final, I got on more ball against Derry than in any other game he had seen me play. But I just gave it away. My kick pass was always one of my assets. It let me down in the final.

The homecoming was muted.

The faithful were still there, waiting for us. I was sombre. Being taken off had affected me. I wondered would I get another chance. Billy was downcast as well. He had been through a lot, fought a lot of battles. A lot of us had a lot to think about before the beginning of the next season.

CHAPTER**14**

The Park.

May 27, 1996.

Lying on a table in the cramped dressing room I feel the needle pierce the tight skin on my forehead.

"I'm going to be sick, Doc."

I'm spending more time with him these days.

He gets out of the way.

I get sick.

He tries again.

A few stitches are inserted.

My stomach is churning like a washing machine.

"Alright, Ted?" Dr Con asks.

Sick again.

And again.

"There's no way you can go back out there," he tells me. He means the second half of the Munster hurling Championship first-round, against Limerick.

"I'll be fine."

There's nothing left in my stomach anyway.

"Just stitch up the head ... and I'll be fine."

Dr Con Murphy: medic, counsellor, comedian, friend.

He finishes stitching and looks around for the manager. I notice he is grim-faced. That's not Con's general demeanour. I know he is serious. He won't let me go back out for the second half.

I stand up.

My legs are wobbly.

My head is spinning a little. I feel weak. Is it a question of fitness or age? I ask myself. On other days, in the past, I would have argued with the Doc. Today, I don't have the energy.

We're leading by a point. I felt alright out there, even immediately after Mike Galligan accidentally split my head open. He was only flicking the ball to Sean O'Neill but the bas of the hurl caught me as I tried to block him. I was momentarily stunned. I lay on the ground getting my bearings. Dr Con came running over.

"I'm alright," I told him. "Can you stop the blood?"

I resumed with a heavy bandage around my head and felt alright. But, when half time was blown about ten minutes later, I was feeling weary. I walked off the field with my head down, blood seeping underneath the bandage.

If I had known it was to be the last time I would make that journey wearing a Cork jersey I might have taken a moment to look around. I might even have allowed myself to be a little sentimental for a change. This place, with its imposing stand and the wide expanse of terracing, had been like a second home to me for ten years.

I had spent an inordinate amount of time there. I had covered every inch of the playing surface. I had fought and bled there. I had walked miles of its corridors. My name had echoed on the walls of committee rooms. All those thoughts came later. I had too much else on my mind. The fact that I might possibly be making a final journey never dawned on me.

In the dressing room I look at the Doc. He is speaking to the management team. Jimmy Barry Murphy, Tom Cashman and Tony O'Sullivan. Three Legends. They'd been appointed the previous autumn to manage the team. This had helped prolong my career at a time when there was a doubt about what would happen next.

Jimmy comes over. He is concerned, even though he has a lot more to think about. We exchange just a few words. When Dr Con gives medical advice we always listen.

My game is over.

I nod in resignation. My great friend Jim Cashman has a quick word and gives me a consolatory pat on the shoulder. I offer him words of encouragement. He files out with the rest of the players. I linger, in no hurry, sore and tired; the strain of 46 career Championship games – 20 hurling, 26 football – etched on my face.

I didn't know it then, but my inter-county career was also about to come to an end.

A few weeks later, I would take a penalty for Glanmire in the Cork football Championship. I'd hear a tear. Ankle ligaments separating.

Season over.

•••••

It annoys me when I hear people say that we should have achieved more as a football team. They forget that, as a general rule, we don't do football All-Irelands in Cork. Just take a look at the history books. Cork have won seven All-Ireland senior football Championships.

We have won 30 hurling Championships.

Our team is the only one in Cork football history to win two Championships. I think that statistic alone proves that we were achievers. We played in four consecutive finals, six in total including a replay, in seven seasons. I think that is an impressive record.

Meath and ourselves completely dominated the game for four years. No one else came close. They won two, we won two. If one or other of us had not been around then we would have won a lot more. But that is what fate decreed for us.

I am very glad to be able to say I won two All-Ireland football medals. There is only a small group of people in Cork who can say that. Jack Lynch won one, so too did Jimmy Barry Murphy. We were a special group. So were the Meath lads.

Football always comes second in Cork. Most of the time, it pales into insignificance compared to hurling. But, for that four-year period between, 1987 and 1990, football was the number one priority in the county. It was an incredible time for everyone, players and supporters.

On the Monday morning after a football All-Ireland you made sure you booked your hotel room for the next year. That was how we lived. We marked the days on the calendar at the start of every year because we knew we had a team good enough to go all the way every year. I have always maintained that in Cork it is easier to win an All-Ireland hurling title because we have so many good hurlers to choose from. In football you have to manufacture a team. During the 1980s, we got the structures right. The Under-21s provided a steady supply of talent and Billy came along at the right time to nurture that talent.

It was important that Larry and Shea came along. They would have made a difference in any county, and I include Kerry in that. If they had switched to Dublin, then Dublin might have won an All-Ireland around that time. They were that good. Larry was unbelievably talented and incredibly dedicated.

I always enjoyed playing with Shea. I was often used at wing-forward and enjoyed that, too. My job out there was to win our own kick outs. That wasn't the most difficult job because John Kerins was so accurate. I hear a lot of talk today about goalkeepers and the fine art of kick outs. None of them are as good as Kerinsy was.

He was one of the dozen players from the 1993 final that had also been part of the squad in 1987. When you consider the injury to Colman Corrigan that cut short his career, and that the likes of Dinny Allen and Dave Barry were a bit older than the rest of us, that is a big number of players to survive during such a highly competitive period.

We had won five Munster titles in seven Championships by the end of 1993. I would add two more to my collection but I had begun slipping down the pecking order the moment I got the finger in Croke Park. I did have one more big day against Kerry. I came on as a substitute and scored two points in The Park in 1994. I also played as a sub in the Munster final against Tipperary.

On August 14, 1994, I played in Croke Park for the last time. I wore the

No.20 jersey and came on for Shea. It was the All-Ireland semi-final against Down. I knew that day that things were changing in Gaelic football. The Down players were huge. They had legs like tree trunks. I had seen them a few years before, played against some of them, and they had grown. The word was that they had changed their training routines completely. I could see that. They must have been lifting some very heavy weights to build up such muscle.

They had some good footballers as well. They won a second All-Ireland that year, to go with the 1991 title. Greg Blaney was an outstanding player. He was also a very good hurler. James McCartan wasn't the biggest guy around but he was strong and quick. Mickey Linden was exceptional.

Their career trajectory was so different to ours. We were a constant presence in the latter stages of the Championship from 1987. Down came in 1991 and went again. They came back in 1994, and that was it. The provincial system was partly the cause. But I think it is due also to our consistency, for which we don't always receive credit.

I might have left the scene after that game but was chosen to play in the National League. I was sent off against Clare but was back playing in the last game of the year at the end of November, against Galway. I scored 1-2. I stayed with the squad and won a seventh Munster medal in 1995, but got no game time against Kerry in Killarney.

The No.22 adorned my back in Croke Park. We played Dublin in the All-Ireland semi-final on August 20, 1995. Only John O'Leary of my buddies from Australia in '86 was still playing with the Dubs. The only Cork player from that trip still keeping me company was John O'Driscoll. I didn't get a run.

Keith Barr was playing. He was much quieter by then. Jason Sherlock was all the rage. He had Cork connections. He actually played some under-age hurling with Ballyhea in Cork. His goal separated the teams, and Hill 16 had a new hero. They serenaded him in song. Dublin went on to win the All-Ireland title. It was their first win since 1983, the year I played in the minor final and chased Brian Mullins and Brian Talty around The Burlington Hotel.

In the disappointment of that loss, we found some solace in the fact that we were still a top-four team after nine years.

I trained over the winter and waited for the warmer days. One evening, early in 1996, Christy Collins from Castletownsend rang. He was the chairman of the selectors. When I heard his voice on the other end of the line I knew. I hadn't made the Championship squad. I was sad but had no ill feeling towards him, Billy or any of the selectors. When I said, "Thanks for everything," to Christy, I meant it.

It had been an incredible time.

It had been my ambition as a kid to play hurling for Cork and to win All-Ireland titles. I like playing football but it wasn't my inspiration. Yet, for twelve years, I had been engulfed in the game. It had provided me with some of my greatest days and provided me with some of my best memories. I met Oonagh through football.

It is hard to believe, while reflecting now, that Kerinsy and Mick Mc are no longer with us. Mick died in a car accident in 1998. He was only 32. He wasn't just a great footballer, he was a great friend. We'd had some good times together, on and off the field.

John had a courageous fight against cancer. He was only 39 when that fight ended. Experience had shown me that life was not fair but this was almost too much.

While completing this book I learned of the tragic death of Paul O'Connor who had played on the hurling team with me a few times. We were at midfield together for the 1988 Championship and Paul also lined out in 1989. Paul was one of the good guys and his death came as a great shock.

•••••

Often I am asked about how I reached the decision to retire or what happened when I retired. The difficulty in finding an answer is that I never actually retired as a Cork footballer or hurler.

I just became surplus to requirements, first with the footballers and then with the hurlers. Nobody gave me a going away present. There was no big announcement. I was available for selection the following year. And the year after that. No one called. I wasn't actually waiting for a call or expecting one. That was the way it should be.

My time was up.

I heard at the time that some players from other counties had been well paid by various national newspapers for an exclusive announcement of their retirement. Fair play to them. No one offered me anything. I probably would have accepted money but I don't know because I never got the chance. But it wasn't something that bothered me. I didn't want a fuss. I wasn't playing for Cork any more. So what? There were lads like Joe Deane in the team at that stage. They're the lads people should have been talking about, not me.

If I'd had a choice I would have preferred to finish on a higher note. The hurlers were well stuffed in the second half of that match against Limerick. Would I have been able to stop the onslaught?

No.

The end had come.

It had actually been coming for a while. A new senior hurling management team had been appointed at the end of 1993 to replace the Padre and Gerald. Johnny Clifford came back. It wasn't a success. We played Limerick in the Championship in 1994 and lost in the first round by three points.

I was taken off at half time. It was becoming a habit. I remained on the panel and trained over the following winter. I was getting to know a lot of younger guys, recognising in them the anxiety and eagerness I myself felt ten years before as a new kid. Brian Corcoran was growing up fast. Timmy Kelleher, Barry Egan, Kevin Murray and Alan Browne were becoming prominent.

From the 1986 squad with whom I began, only Ger Cunningham, Jim Cashman, Tomas Mulcahy and Tony O'Sullivan remained for the 1995 Championship. And we were beginning to show signs of wear and tear, on and off the field. I was picking up little injuries. So was Tomas. A lot of changes were being made in personnel but there was no sign of coherence, of a certainty about what shape the team was taking.

Still, I remember sitting in the Mackey Stand in the Gaelic Grounds on the first Sunday in June and being confident that Cork had a team good enough to beat a young Clare team. I thought I would have been fit enough to play but was ruled out on the day of the game. Tomas was sitting beside me in the stand. We watched as Ollie Baker scored a late goal for Clare to win the game. Both of us looked at each other. We sensed the end was nigh.

Then the Cork county board did something very sensible. Jimmy Barry Murphy had been the minor manager in 1995 and they had won the All-Ireland title. He was promoted to senior manager and had Tom Cashman and Tony O'Sullivan appointed as his selectors.

They brought in Kevin Kehily, the former Cork football star, to look after the physical training of the team. They also began to introduce some of the minors, including Sean Og O hAilpin. I began to enjoy training again. Jimmy gave me plenty of encouragement. He needed my physical presence and my work-rate. As the 1996 Championship loomed, I assumed some of the responsibility of a senior player.

We were ambushed by a Limerick team that was more experienced. They had been in the All-Ireland final in 1994 and should have won it. Players like Ciaran Carey and Gary Kirby were amongst the best in the game at the time. And still we were ahead at half time, 1-5 to 0-7. We had displayed inexperience by the number of wides we struck in the first half and Ger had to make a couple of very good saves.

Joe Quaid also made one very good save for Limerick. Would it have made any difference if that ball had gone in? We'll never know. It's one of the great things about sport, the little things upon which fate is decreed.

Limerick tore into Cork in the second half. We added just another three points. They belted in 3-11. It was Cork's worst defeat in sixty years and it was also the first time Cork had lost a hurling Championship game in The Park. It was a tough start in management for Jimmy. I think he made a few decisions in the aftermath, including about my future.

I wasn't invited back. Some months later I heard a panel for the next season had been announced and was printed in the *Examiner*. My name wasn't on it. A while later a letter arrived from the county board.

Thank for your years of service, words to that effect.

It was time to move on, to hand the jersey over to the next guy. You are only a temporary custodian. Many have gone before you and many will come after you. That's the way it was and still is, and I am happy with that.

Jimmy, Tom and Tony knew they had to build. They would dip into the pool of talented youngsters. I had played my part in 1996 in providing a physical presence as well as some leadership. They went on to the next stage and I was not on board. It would take them a few years to build a new team and I would watch with interest from afar.

Slowly over the next three years, they created a completely new team. It wasn't easy. They had to contend with a very competitive Munster Championship in which Clare and Limerick were very strong, and Waterford were beginning to make an impact. But they eventually got the right blend and won the Championship in 1999. It was a new era. Ours was done with.

I have no regrets. How could I have? My first Championship game was an All-Ireland final which we won. I had played with some of the greatest hurlers ever to grace the game. I have no intention of choosing favourites. The list is endless. They have all been mentioned somewhere in this book.

In a way, I was looking forward to looking in from the outside. Cork's stock was low at the time but I knew that there was some serious talent coming through. It might take a few years but we wouldn't be down for too long. I had some first-hand experience of the new talent from my final days with the county and from the club scene. Our team at Sarsfields was ageing a little but we were still very competitive. We battled our way to the county final in 1997. A familiar sight awaited us, the Imokilly hurlers.

They had a few youngsters in the team, Donal Og Cusack, Diarmuid O'Sullivan, Timmy McCarthy and Mark Landers amongst them. I suspected we would be hearing a lot more about them in the future.

We lost.

I had a good innings with both the club and the county.

I had no regrets. Those came later.

CHAPTER 15

NO ONE TO BLAME BUT MYSELF

Oonagh left me in 2003.

She brought the three children with her back to her native Passage. We were officially separated four years later.

There it is.

In black and white.

The hardest three sentences I have ever had to utter. Reading them I feel as if I am suffocating. Even now, nine years after she left our home, I have failed to come to terms with it.

I have made mistakes in life and there are a few things I regret. But nothing compares to how I feel about the break-up of our marriage. I made a mess of it. I have no one to blame but myself.

It was too late to turn back the clock, the day she moved her possessions out of our home in Glanmire. But every morning to this day I wake and wish that I had the opportunity to put things right, to get back to when we were happy and able to live together as husband and wife, with our family around us.

She left because she had to. I wasn't there for her and she needed me. I had become lost in my own selfish world. By the time I realised the extent to which I had distanced myself from real life responsibilities she had already suffered enough.

It is hard to pinpoint exactly when the problems began. It was a gradual process during which there were a number of triggers. The most obvious trigger was the end of my career with the Cork hurlers and footballers. Maybe I should have confided in someone at the time; by the time I realised it was causing me problems it was already too late. Only in recent years, when trying to come to terms with the worst years of my life, have I been able to make sense of the place I found myself in when I no longer existed within the bubble of the inter-county GAA star. I did continue to play with the club for a few years and that kept the lid on the pressure-cooker. But, when I stopped playing completely, when the bubble burst and I was let out into the real world, I found that I was unable to cope. I remember when I worked for my brother-in-law, Peter Holland, we used to let newborn calves out into the field. They would run wild. That was me out of my bubble.

The bubble took a while to burst completely. I was still working in Beamish & Crawford and that provided me with a certain structure outside the home. Oonagh and I had opened a pub in the centre of Glanmire and it was going well. She was a natural at the job. She was good with people and they were very fond of her. "She's dynamite," they would say to me when I would arrive in the evening after a day at work.

Sinead was born in 1999. We had our two boys and now a baby girl. It was almost perfect. The truth is I was even struggling at that time. It might have looked to everyone else as if I had the world at my feet. I had just completed a very successful career as a sportsman, I had a job and a new business, and a lovely young family. Deep down, however, I was not coping at all, well away from the safe confines of inter-county hurling and football.

I had lived an adult life of discipline and restraint. Of course, I enjoyed a few drinks and socialising, but when I was playing for Cork I had very little time for anything other than training and playing. I didn't keep contact with many of my friends. It wasn't my fault or their fault, just the circumstances. Saturday night was the night for socialising. I was usually getting ready for a match so I wasn't out.

It never bothered me because there were compensations. Apart from the satisfaction of playing sport at the highest level and of winning big games every year, I was part of two groups of young men who were treated in a privileged manner. Our lives were different to those of other twenty-somethings around Cork.

We lived in the spotlight for more than ten years. It was a time of real change in Ireland and in the GAA. Before that you could have lived in relative anonymity except for the day of a game. But the media interest in hurling and football during the decade I played with Cork grew substantially. The media itself grew. Gaelic games were big news and so the players found themselves in the news.

You know what it's like when you come home from a holiday? It takes a few days to wind down, to get used to normal life again. Well, I had been living in a sort of suspended reality for ten years and when I got back to reality I found it took me a very long time to adjust. Some players adjust easily. I was one of the many who don't.

There is an element of selfishness about the life of a sportsman or woman competing at the top of their chosen discipline. It is a necessary ingredient for success. Hurling and football soaked up that selfishness. When I gave up, the selfishness manifested itself in a different way. I thought of myself and myself alone. I forgot about others.

I forgot about Oonagh.

I had also lived to a schedule for most of my life. Every morning I knew what was mapped out for my day. I went to work and then I went hurling or kicking football. My coaches decided my life's itinerary. I knew virtually hour by hour what I would be doing with my life. It was a sort of comfort zone. I didn't have time to fill and I didn't have too many decisions to make.

The season then was never-ending. I played in an All-Ireland final every year between 1986 and 1993 – with the exception of 1991 – so I was involved in the Championship until September. The League began in October. I would play right into December with the county or the club and, after a short break at Christmas, we would be back playing tournament games in January.

From the age of about 15, I didn't know anything different. And then, around 1999, I was handed a new form of freedom. It was a normal life for most people but it was not normal to me.

There was a huge void in my life. I know now how I should have filled it. I should have spent the time with my family. Instead I invested emotionally in my own needs. I had never had the freedom of a young man, able to spend a few hours in the pub or the snooker hall without responsibility. I did it then, forgetting that I had responsibilities at home.

Being married to a footballer or hurler is never easy. We have to make great sacrifices when we are playing and that means your partner must also make sacrifices. We would attend big award ceremonies and these were supposed to be precious evenings together. But when I turned up to these awards or whatever I spent most of my time chatting with other players, fellas I wouldn't see except on the pitch.

The girls, Oonagh and the other wives and girlfriends, would often point out that we weren't paying attention to them. I know I would always reply that if I didn't talk to people they would think I had a big head.

We were being led everywhere as players and I went willingly.

When the playing days were over, I was still in demand but it was not conducive to family life. I presented medals all over the country – I was in Carlow one night, Cavan the next. I didn't know how to say no. I was being treated like a star. Christ, you'd have thought it was Hollywood at times.

When it was all over Oonagh had every right to expect me to be at home. But, when 6pm came and I had nothing else to do, I went to the pub. Not my own pub, of course, somewhere else.

We were young and busy and got through the first few years. Then there was a second trigger. We decided to build a new, bigger pub.

It was 1999 and the developer, Owen O'Callaghan, announced a major new commercial centre would be built just down the road, in Riverstown. Included was a site for a public house. It got me thinking. It was a chance for us to better ourselves and it was also a little about survival.

We were running a small pub in the centre of a village with no parking on the street. A new pub was going to be opened less than a mile away. It was reasonable to assume that the new pub would have an adverse effect on our business.

I spoke to Owen O'Callaghan. He was very courteous to me. He understood my position. I also had an advantage: I already had a licence and since the new premises was located less than a mile from my current premises it was possible to transfer the licence. We did a deal and I had plans drawn up for a 5,000 square metre public house, with an off licence attached and further plans for a restaurant upstairs.

There were some people who said I should have stayed where I was. Small is beautiful and all that. But I was a young man who saw an opportunity to move on in life. I made the move for the right reasons. Unfortunately, I was not in the right place in my own life to do it. I wouldn't have made the move if I had thought it would lead to the break-up of our marriage.

There was also a conflict of interest with my day job. After fourteen years, I left Beamish & Crawford. They had been quite happy and were accommodating when we ran a small village pub. But now that we were expanding and would be dealing with a greater number of suppliers, and much greater quantities, it was not feasible for me to remain as a sales person for one brewery.

I loved the old job. Years later, when I heard the news that it would be closed, I cried. I'd had brilliant days there and brilliant colleagues.

So now I didn't have football, hurling, or Beamish & Crawford. I did have a new pub. And I had all the pressures that brings. Emotionally I ran away. I handed over the responsibility for the business and the family to Oonagh.

We opened the Ghlaise Bhui, named after the river in which I played as a boy. Some people advised me to use my own name, to cash in on the fame I had gained as a hurler and footballer. But I was never comfortable with that sort of celebrity connection. I was afraid it might suggest that I had become big headed or something. That is another indicator of my mindset at the time.

The new pub was a success. But it broke us physically and mentally. I wasn't there enough. I would get up in the morning, have a few slices of bread, some cheese and a glass of water and I was gone. I didn't want to know about problems. There was a lot of pressure running a business of that size and I couldn't cope with it. Again, I ran away. I was drinking too much. I didn't give Oonagh enough time or support.

Gradually, we began to drift apart even though I didn't notice it. Of course I knew that we had difficulties, but I walked away from them, too. I was living in my own world and it wasn't real. I just did my own thing. I was selfish.

I never saw what was coming down the track. I didn't want to. So, when Oonagh told me she was leaving, I was shocked. I couldn't come to terms with it. Yes, there had been strains but I truly never thought that it would come to this. It took me a while to realise what I had done. I wanted to make things right between us, but I had left it too late. She had to get out of the marriage for her own sake.

I was angry and sad. I will never forget the day she moved out. I can still hear the door closing. I begged her to stay. I was crying like a baby. I couldn't cope with it. I kept saying sorry and asking her to give me a chance.

But she had to go.

I realise that now.

When I got separated it was like a death in the family. I had lost my father, my brother, my brother-in-law. My sister was permanently hospitalised. But nothing had hit me like this. It was the end of something that I never thought would end.

My three beautiful kids were gone. The woman I thought would be with me forever was gone. I could never envisage being with anyone else. I never will be.

I blame myself.

It is very hard to talk about, to put these words onto paper. I have never reconciled myself to what happened. It still upsets me. It was tough. I am so fond of her family. I suppose I have never moved on.

I have always hoped that we would get back together. Even now. I know it's not going to happen after all these years but some mornings I wake up and the hope is back. It's not rational but it is there.

It was an awful time, very rough emotionally and physically. I wouldn't wish it on my worst enemy. I'm not looking for sympathy. I am where I am and I put myself in this position. No one else did it. But it was tougher still when the solicitors became involved. I hated that part of it intensely.

Oonagh has her own home now in Passage. She has done a brilliant job with the kids. Any acrimony between myself and herself has long since gone. We get on well. Cian and Niall are both working here in Cork. Niall is thinking about continuing his studies and would like to join the Gardai. Sinead is in secondary school.

The three of them are involved in the GAA. Cian and Niall play hurling with Sarsfields and football with Passage. Sinead is also involved with Passage.

Cian had been getting a few headlines himself for his exploits as a hurler. I was a proud man when he played for Cork in the Championship in 2012. It hasn't been easy for him. He came into the Cork set-up during the strike of 2009. That was hard. But he stuck at it and he got his reward.

I am nervous watching him. I puck every ball. I give out. Why isn't he in a certain position, why isn't he doing this or that? I play every part of it. He will ask me how he has done and I will tell him. Sometimes, I'm too straight but at least that way he knows I won't tell him any lies. He has been very dedicated and deserves to get a good run with the team.

He is taking the long-range frees now as well. That shows he is growing in confidence. He has been part of the Sarsfields team that won two Cork senior Championships in four years. He scored eight points in the 2010 final against Glen Rovers and won the Man of the Match award. That's something his father never did!

I missed the three children terribly when Oonagh and I separated. The house has felt empty ever since.

I had tried to fill my time in those years after my career ended by taking up golf but it just never appealed to me. From time to time I enjoyed it but, overall, I didn't find it rewarding. I don't have the patience for it. I wasn't willing to put in the time to get what I wanted from it. It is a very time-consuming sport and I couldn't see myself every Saturday or Sunday getting up at 7am and teeing off at 7.30 and being back home for 11am. That's not enjoyment for me. I wanted to be able to go out whenever I felt like it and play eight or nine holes but I found I couldn't always get out on a course. You work to a timetable dictated by the timesheet and that was not for me.

We sold the pub in 2003. I drifted for a couple of years. I was lucky to get involved in coaching. It helped keep me sane. Away from the hurling field I was in a bad place. The 'Dual Star' headlines returned. Only, this time, they weren't too pleasant.

•••••

"GAA Star to Appeal in Drink-driving Case"
Front page.

I didn't even get that sort of coverage in 1990.

I was accustomed to the jostling of photographers and looking into TV cameras during the month of September when I was a player. It was a pleasure. In September of 2007, it was a bloody nuisance.

In Cobh District Court I had been sentenced to two months in jail and fined €1,150 after being found guilty of dangerous driving and refusing to give Gardai a blood or urine sample. Judge Michael Patwell said I had given "the two fingers" to the law.

I had denied the charges, which arose after I was stopped in Glanmire in November of 2006. I insisted that I had not been drinking and that I had not been driving dangerously. The Garda did not agree.

The court was told that I had demanded to be tested with a breathaliser, or intoxiliser as it is known in law. That test wasn't available so, by law, I was refusing to supply a blood or urine sample. I didn't know that at the time.

Two months in jail!

Crazy stuff.

When I arrived at Cobh courthouse that morning, it was just another day for the judge and the solicitors. People drifted in and out of the courthouse as various cases were called and dealt with. There were a few journalists in court, one face was vaguely familiar. I thought nothing of it. A few people gave me a second glance. One or two said, "hello". Judge Patwell announced a break for lunch.

I saw the first photographer as I walked towards the door of the courthouse. Then I saw the TV cameras. People stepped aside. I was like a rabbit in headlights.

Hollywood again.

Except there was no red carpet.

When court resumed you could sense the change in atmosphere. It was no longer a routine day at court. It was drama.

The Garda gave his evidence. I gave mine. Judge Patwell wasn't impressed with me. It didn't help that a few minutes later I thought court was over and turned on my mobile phone. It rang immediately. Judge Patwell was even less pleased with me.

Even though I "vehemently" denied, as one newspaper reported, driving dangerously and that I explained that I did not understand the consequences of refusing to give the sample when a breathaliser test wasn't available, I received a two month jail sentence.

The coverage, inevitable though it was, was crazy. I thought the sentence was, too. I don't condone drink driving. No one should get behind the wheel of a car when they are drunk. I do believe that a man can have a pint or two in his local and drive home. But that's it.

But there was a sense that I should have been ashamed; that I had brought shame on my family. There is a stigma attached to being charged with drink-driving. Well, I wasn't ashamed. I wasn't exactly proud of being involved in such a case but I felt no shame.

Because of who I was the whole thing became a circus. It was on the TV news at 6pm that evening. It was on the radio and was covered by all the newspapers.

Front page: Teddy the villain.

I wasn't a villain. I made a mistake. I felt the price I was told I would have to pay for that mistake was out of proportion. There were men who had done a lot worse than I had and they hadn't faced the prospect of jail.

At the Cork Circuit Appeals Court at the end of May, 2008, Judge Patrick Moran removed the jail term, fined me €750 and banned me from driving for two years.

CHAPTER16

STRIKE OUT

Being the stubborn man that I am, I've had my share of disagreements with GAA officials and team managers in Cork over the course of my playing career. Once, I even refused to play for the football team because I felt I was being punished for playing for my club.

That was a short dispute at the end of 1992, resolved through a one-to-one negotiation with Billy. Neither of us would be short-listed for the role of peacekeeper, but we managed to settle our differences for the overall good of the team.

I always felt that, as a county footballer and hurler, I was well looked after by the Cork county board and its secretary, Frank Murphy. Elsewhere on these pages, I have said that we were privileged people as players. I felt it was a privilege for me to represent Cork, but I also felt that we received preferential treatment, and I was grateful.

Worryingly, the rumblings of discontent amongst those who succeeded us as Cork hurlers became louder and louder as 2002 came to a close. I was also surprised by the content of the complaints and the apparent failure of the authorities in the county to provide what were really basic needs for any team competing at the highest level.

Generally, we keep our arguments in Cork private. This argument was different because it went public immediately. If the complaints the players were making were justified then I felt the board had a case to answer and would have to respond.

Although I was no longer involved in the county set-up, I had a fair idea of what was happening. Bertie Og Murphy, a Sarsfields man and former teammate of mine, was managing the Cork hurlers. Bertie Og always set the highest standards as a player and as a coach. I was confident he would be able to bring the dispute between the players and the board to a resolution, eventually.

I never thought the players would use the nuclear option of withdrawing their services. What became known as the first players' strike was a shock to the system. The biggest victim became Bertie Og. As the dispute rumbled on, he felt he had no option but to resign. It was an absolute shame that a good man was forced into such a position.

Little did I realise that the next time the players would stage a revolt I would find myself in the middle of it all, watching from the inside, as so much damage was inflicted to the heart and soul of the GAA in Cork that it will take years for the Association to recover.

As I reflect on that terrible period, I am more convinced than ever that the players put their own interests ahead of the greater good of the game of hurling and the GAA in Cork.

At the time, I predicted that Cork hurling would be damaged for the next ten years. We are already almost halfway through that time and look at what has happened: We have won nothing.

Cork hurling is badly fractured. Families are still displaying wounds from that civil war. Clubs were split. Communities were divided and have yet to recover. People who had dedicated their lives to Cork hurling have walked away, never to return. They gave freely of their time and energy to create an environment, in every corner of Cork, in which young boys and girls could learn the game and play to the highest possible standard. And they felt betrayed.

That is the legacy of this generation of Cork hurling. It won't be remembered by everyone for the glorious days when it won three All-Ireland Championships, nor for the victories over Kilkenny and Galway. It will be remembered by many for the strikes that ripped the heart and soul out of something that we all loved together.

It all began in late 2007.

I remember taking a phone call. It was from the GAA offices in Pairc Ui Chaoimh. I was asked would I be willing to let my name go forward for ratification as a selector with the Cork football team for the following year. Teddy Holland, against whom I had played football at club level, was to be nominated as team manager.

Also appointed as selectors were Liam Hodnett, Diarmuid O'Donovan and Mick O'Loughlin. I knew them and felt we would make a good team.

I also spoke to Teddy. It had been mentioned to me that some of the players were unhappy that Teddy had not chosen his own selectors. Part of the agreement which had ended the 2002 strike was that the manager could choose his selectors. The Cork board had voted to revert to the old system and the players were upset.

Teddy assured me that there was nothing to worry about. He was happy for the board to pick his selectors and he was pleased that they had chosen the four of us. That sounded good to me. If Teddy Holland was happy, then it shouldn't be a problem.

Shortly afterwards, however, it became obvious that there was a problem. A big one. The players asked us to meet them. Graham Canty, Anthony Lynch, Pearse O'Neill and Daniel Goulding were four of the players' representatives. They told us they wanted us to resign.

Straight up.

They wanted us out.

I wanted to know why. I wanted them to tell me what I had done wrong. I had no issues with them. I was a former player who'd had no involvement with any of these players before. I wanted them to explain what their problem with me was. Where was all this coming from?

They couldn't, or wouldn't, give me an answer. That annoyed me.

I had been a player with Cork. I knew what it was like. I wanted to work with these guys, to help them become successful. And here they were, before we had even had a training session together, telling us they wanted us to resign.

Their only problem, they said, was that we had not been chosen by Teddy. The fact that he was happy with us as his selectors didn't impress them at all.

It became obvious that there was a different, bigger, issue than the selection committee. Some players decided they didn't want Teddy Holland as coach. I never found out why. Some had played with the Cork minor team managed by him. Did something happen then? Not according to Teddy Holland.

Around the county at the time, no one seemed to have the stomach for another strike. I didn't detect a lot of sympathy for the footballers. They didn't have a cause worth fighting for. They were in trouble.

The hurlers came riding along on their chargers in support. Suddenly, the conflict became a war.

The footballers would never have received the volume of support they eventually enjoyed without having the hurlers with them. And I believe this was the first salvo to be fired by the hurlers in their attempt, a year later, to get rid of Gerald McCarthy as their own manager.

What followed over the next two years was sad. It was also unnecessary. Teddy Holland was the next victim. A good man volunteering for a demanding role for the glory and honour of his county was treated disgracefully.

Gerald McCarthy, one of the legends of hurling, the holder of five All-Ireland medals who had captained his county to All-Ireland success while still a teenager, was portrayed as someone completely out of his depth, and worse. For that alone the players' side should hang their heads in shame.

Kieran Mulvey, the highly thought of and competent Chairman of the Labour Relations Commission was brought in to try and help resolve the row, though I personally believed the dispute should have been dealt with internally.

The Mulvey process concluded with a recommendation that the manager and his four selectors should step down.

I refused.

I had done nothing wrong.

There were other concessions made to the players: It was agreed that the players would have two representatives on the committees that would choose future managers. In return, the players signed a document agreeing not to strike in the future. For them that was the cost of winning the war. But the agreement didn't hold.

We didn't even enjoy a year of peace. By Christmas of 2008, another civil war had broken out, and this one was even more bitter, causing deep wounds and divisions that exist to this day.

I had no hesitation in accepting Gerald McCarthy's invitation to become one of his selectors when he was reappointed as Cork senior hurling manager for a two-year term that would take in the 2009 and 2010 Championships. I loved being involved with teams. I knew Gerald well, and he had been our coach when we won the All-Ireland Championship in 1990.

Also, I was familiar with the players. I had played against some of them towards the end of my career and I had coached teams in the Cork Championship. There was a good mix of senior players along with some young talent.

I was not aware of the militant dynamic that existed in the squad. Their inclination to do their own thing came as a surprise.

The players did not want Gerald as their manager. Gerald managed the team the way he thought it should be managed. He did not allow the players to dictate what should be done. They didn't like that. They wanted to control things by choosing their own man.

What followed was a protracted battle from which there could be no winners. The reputation of a great hurling man was tarnished by supporters of the hurlers' stance. There are certain things that are easy to forgive but I cannot forgive those people for what they said about Gerald and for how they tried to portray him. It was an assault on the character and reputation of one of the great men of hurling.

It was as if Gerald McCarthy was being blamed for every defeat, while the players got the credit for every victory.

It was nonsense.

Frank Murphy became a target for much verbal abuse. He was portrayed in a less than pleasant light. Naturally, when Frank's brilliant administrative mind was of use to the players they were happy to forget about their perceived problems with him and were happy to lean on his sturdy shoulder.

I didn't have a problem with players looking for better conditions. I believed the formation of the Gaelic Players' Association was potentially very positive, if they focussed on player welfare.

I did have a big problem with the players demanding the right to choose their own manager or having a veto over whoever the county board appointed to the post. That could not be allowed. That the players made an attempt to get that power of veto, convinced me they were living in a fantasy world.

Things got out of control. The players had a crowd behind them and that gave them strength. The GAA bent the knee towards them. The Director General of the GAA, Paraic Duffy, became involved. We know now that he had meetings with representatives of the players. I think that was a mistake.

We tried to do the jobs we were democratically elected to do. We didn't have the best players in Cork available to us so we chose the next in line. These were brave young men. Emotions were raw at this time. The hurlers who agreed to play were subjected to abuse on the street, at work and when socialising.

They were telephoned regularly. Pressure was applied to them not to play. They were not deterred. I was proud of them. My son Cian played. I was proud of him, too. Most of these guys knew that when the strike was over they would not be playing for Cork but they were willing to play their part to ensure that Cork teams fulfilled their commitments.

My fear was that this would escalate. It was a bad time. A lot of people were hurt. Many turned away and never returned. Friendships were fractured. Brothers fought with each other. Fathers and sons fell out.

The players ran a good PR campaign. They presented themselves as passionate about Cork hurling. The thing about passion is that you have to handle it properly.

Any player's time as a Cork hurler is only temporary. That was as true for the players opposing us as it was for me when I was a player. They had inherited the jersey from those who had gone before them and, in time, they would hand on the jersey to the next generation. I felt that value was overlooked by some.

They traded on the fact that they had won three All-Ireland titles. There's nothing very unusual about that in Cork. Gerald had won five and he had coached another team to an All-Ireland win. But some people were going around mocking him and saying he didn't know what he was doing.

They claimed they were acting out of love for Cork hurling. All the row did was damage Cork hurling. Today, we're still living with the effects of it.

CHAPTER **17**

MY REFUGE

I still find refuge at the GAA pitch.

These days I don't have to go there to hide from my sisters!

There's nothing I enjoy more than strolling down to the pitch in the evening to watch a game. I'll watch the kids and the adults. I tend to choose hurling these days. It was always my first choice anyway, and I just don't like the way football is played today.

The GAA pitch is where everything started for me. Sarsfields Hurling Club and Glanmire Gaelic Football Club created my identity. They are two separate entities representing the one community.

The pitches, like the locality, have changed dramatically since those days at the start of the 1970s, when I first scampered around excitedly under the watchful eyes of Mickey Barry, Tadhgy Murphy and Paddy Duggan.

In those days, the clubs shared the same facilities in Glanmire, meagre as the facilities were then. The priority was the pitches and I recall them being in pristine condition all year round, despite heavy usage. Our repertoire was not confined solely to hurling and football. We played rounders and called it cricket. James Halligan coached us in that fine art. We held athletics meetings and cycle races. Billy O'Mahony encouraged us to try the high jump. The first evening he came to coach us the lads took to it with great gusto. They simply ran at the bar in a straight line and jumped over it like you would jump a wall or a ditch.

I watched 10 or 15 of them do it. Then it came to my turn. I ran in from the side, and straddled the bar by stretching my body out wide. It wasn't the Fosbury Flop or anything close to it. We wouldn't have known what that was at the time anyway. But it was an attempt that showed I thought differently about my approach. Billy was impressed.

Older men watching my effort nodded knowingly. I was only a young teenager but already my ability to spring off the ground and reach heights others could not was being noticed.

The GAA was woven into the fabric of society. The GAA in Cork had then, and has still, a reputation for being austere, inward looking and locked in tradition. But it was and is far more progressive than that, in many ways. Sure, it has faults, but it has served its community very well.

For example, there were lots of small clubs around Cork in the 1960s, 70s and 80s who, because of low population or lack of resources, were unable to field under-age teams. If boys wanted to play hurling or football, or both, they didn't have an outlet. So, the GAA introduced a rule that allowed them to play for a neighbouring parish.

That presented a problem. Once the boy played under-age for one club a mechanism had to be put in place to ensure he could return to his home club when he left the juvenile ranks. So clubs like ours that took in players from neighbouring parishes registered new juvenile clubs. Glanmire became Glanmire Rovers, Sarsfields became Riverstown.

It made it much less complicated then for the boy to return to his original club. That also ensured that the smaller clubs remained in existence.

We didn't have any facilities in those days. Today the young men and women who play there have the very best facilities. Sarsfields has a modern clubhouse and bar, dressing rooms, a hurling wall, a gym. It is typical of what GAA clubs all over Ireland have created within their communities.

In the middle of the 1980s, Glanmire developed its own facilities in nearby Sally Brook. It caused tension in the community at the time but we can see now that the move showed great foresight from those behind it

Mickey Barry was one of the first people to recognise the need for more pitches. It was he who found the land where the Glanmire club is now located, and negotiated the purchase from the Dooley family. It was a move that many people opposed at the time. Sarsfields and Glanmire had separate executive committees but a shared finance committee. There was a fear in Sarsfields that the financial pressure of the purchase and maintenance of new pitches would be too great.

Now, however, everyone accepts it was good business. More recently, Glanmire has developed two more fields at a place known as Buck Leary's Cross to cater for the ever-increasing numbers playing football.

The provision of such facilities is one of the great achievements of the GAA. In most cases, there has been state assistance through the National Lottery. But it takes more than money to create what we have in clubs like Sarsfields and Glanmire. It takes effort, commitment and pride. It takes community spirit.

That is why I am worried. All of that effort and pride is at risk because the GAA, at a very influential level, is displaying signs that it has forgotten its roots. It is abandoning the very thing that has made it such a great institution – its identity.

There is a proposal emanating from the most powerful body within the GAA, the Central Council, to allow Croke Park and six other major grounds in the country to be used for the staging of the 2023 Rugby Union World Cup. I will be actively campaigning to ensure that it does not happen.

It is madness. If this is allowed to happen it will set a very dangerous precedent that will be a direct threat to the future of hurling and Gaelic football. What will be next – our club grounds? And then we will have nothing.

I am not scaremongering and I am not being blinkered. We allowed Croke Park to be opened to rugby and soccer during the reconstruction of Lansdowne Road. We were told then that it was a one-off. The rule that governs the use of our facilities was modified in a careful manner to safeguard against any further erosion of protection.

Now, those who are supposed to be leading the Association, are advising the members to make further concessions that will benefit only those with whom we are in direct competition.

I don't have a ban mentality and I don't dislike rugby and soccer. I played soccer as a kid and I enjoyed it immensely. I still attend rugby matches from time to time and enjoy the physicality of the game. I would be delighted to see the World Cup played in Ireland, but not if it damages the two sports in which I am involved.

I like soccer and rugby. I am delighted that kids are playing those games. But my games are Gaelic Games and my job is to get the kids playing those games, to make them more attractive than other games.

Rugby and soccer have their own attractions. Amongst those are the international element and the potential for a professional career. The GAA cannot offer either of those so it must utilise its other strengths.

One of the greatest strengths is the facilities we have in the GAA. Why should we be facilitating other sports, popularising them to the extent that it could damage our long-term future?

This is about business.

We are in the business of promoting our own games and in that business our competition is soccer and rugby. Can you imagine the guy in the Texaco station in Glanmire letting the Esso franchise holder in to use his pumps? Or Coca-Cola giving access to its plants to Pepsi? Of course not. Why should it be any different in sport?

When the GAA agreed to open Croke Park for a limited period I expressed concerns. They centred solely on precedent. I understood there was a need to make a gesture of solidarity and agreed to the amendment of the rule on the basis that it was for a limited time and would not lead to any further relaxation of the rule.

Now, we are being asked to open up another six grounds. Who can assure me now that, in another five years, the authorities won't come along and seek another modification? It will be the European Championships, or something like that next.

Those who argue that, because we are content to stage concerts or American football games in our grounds, we should allow soccer and rugby in, are missing the point completely. We are not in competition with American sports. We are not in competition with pop stars. We are in competition with soccer and rugby.

People argue that the GAA will receive massive sums of money to spend on the stadiums to make them ready for the World Cup and that the GAA will, in the long-term, be the big beneficiary in all of this. How can that be when the stadiums no longer belong to you? Because that is what is happening: we are handing over control.

•••••

In any spare time I could find during my playing days I would wander down to the GAA field in the evening and help coach some of the young hurlers. I got great enjoyment from it and knew that I would like to become a coach when my playing days ended. That time came a lot more quickly than I intended, and at a stage in my life when I needed something to distract me from the bad things that were happening.

After reaching the county final in 1997 and losing to Imokilly, the fortunes of the Sarsfields senior team had quickly declined. A lot of the players were at the end of our careers in '97 and, when we stopped playing, the numbers coming through to replace us were insufficient. It is always easy to find coaches when a club is successful. When you go through a few years without success it becomes more difficult to find people prepared to take on what is a very difficult and time-consuming job.

That was the situation facing Sarsfields when we held our annual general meeting at the end of 2002. Quite simply, there was no one who wanted to manage the senior hurling team. I was asked would I let my name go forward. It wasn't something I had expected to happen at that time. I had thought that I would wait another few years working with under-age teams before I would be ready for the senior job.

However, I was appointed and I formed a management team with Tommy Murphy and Mick Mangan, and set about changing routines and structures, as well as attitudes. I put together what I had learned from Fr O'Brien, Gerald McCarthy, Johnny Clifford and Billy Morgan and began to impose all that discipline and order.

It was hard work. Players were asked to change their approach, to accept new challenges, to alter the way they were accustomed to training and playing. I was hard on them. It is always hard for all involved when you are reorganising a team.

Pat Ryan was 27 at the time and one of the most experienced players we had. We also had a good crop of young players coming through from the Under-21 team, including Kieran Murphy and Michael Cussen. Sarsfields won the Cork Under-21 Championship in 2003 and our climb back to the top had begun.

In our first Championship, in 2003, we reached the county semi-final but lost by three points to Blackrock. It was a satisfactory start but we wanted more. We were drawn against Newtownshandrum in the first round of the 2004 Championship and were beaten. Through the qualifier system we got a second chance and reached the semi-final when Newtown awaited us again.

They beat us after a replay and went on to win the All-Ireland club title, in March of 2005. By then, my reign with Sarsfields was coming to an end. For reasons that I have never established, the players had come to the conclusion that they would be better off with a different manager.

Unknown to me, they held a meeting together and then approached the club executive. When I knew I wasn't wanted, I got out of there. There were plenty of people looking for the job then. A couple of barren seasons proved that management was not quite as easy as some people thought.

Meanwhile, I was busy. I coached Killeagh for a year and was then asked to take on Tallow in Waterford. We reached a county semi-final but lost to Lismore.

I was pleased when Bertie Og Murphy took over Sarsfields for 2007. Bertie Og and the Murphy family are Sarsfields people, through and through. He was a dual player with Cork and had done brilliant work with juvenile teams at the club for almost 20 years. He managed the Cork hurlers in 2002 and was the first victim of player power in the county.

Bertie Og helped the team reach a quarter-final in his first year in charge where they lost to Fermoy. I was approached to become a selector in 2008 and was delighted to work with Bertie Og. My own son Cian won a Cork minor medal with Sarsfields in 2007, and was promoted to the senior team by Bertie Og, in 2008. In his first season, Cian won an honour that had eluded me in my own career, a Cork senior hurling Championship medal, when Sars beat Bride Rovers in the final.

We reached the final again in 2009 where we lost to Newtownshandrum. Bertie Og stepped down as manager and I went with him. John Crowley, who had coached Sars to county minor and Under-21 Championship success, was the natural replacement. He steered them right back to the summit and they won a second title in three years. It was a phenomenal time for the club and I was immensely proud to watch Cian and his teammates achieve so much.

You might think that after all those years of playing, coaching and general involvement I might have wanted a rest. But I love the involvement. The Bandon club made contact with me at the start of 2010 to see if I would be interested in coaching their intermediate team. I liked the people involved and agreed.

We reached the county quarter-final that year and then went all the way to win the county intermediate title in 2011. That meant we were promoted to Premier intermediate status for 2012 and the players responded brilliantly. In just our first year we reached the county final where, on October 7, we narrowly lost to Ballinhassig by four points, 1-15 to 1-19. My acute disappointment on the day was tempered by the effort the players gave and by the fact that Sarsfields, with Cian to the fore, won the club's third Cork senior hurling title in five years.

I combined my first two years with Bandon with a spell as a Cork Under-21 hurling selector. My old teammate Ger Fitzgerald was appointed manager for 2010 and 2011, and I was delighted to become part of his team. My previous involvement with Cork teams is detailed elsewhere in this book. I enjoyed the Under-21 experience much more.

•••••

Soon after my appointment as Laois hurling manager, in October 2011, one of the more senior players approached me. I won't name him because he spoke to me in confidence. He asked me to try to convince seven of his former teammates to return to the squad.

For reasons never made absolutely clear to me, apart from what was described as friction between the players and the GAA authorities in Laois, these players had withdrawn from the squad prior to my arrival. I had spoken to some of them and asked them to reconsider. I had phoned them later but they had not taken my calls and did not respond to voicemails.

I explained this to the player. He told me he understood the position I was in but asked me to, "please, just try once more".

I told him, "If I have to go down on my knees and beg them to come back, or if I try to force them to come back, they will be no good to us anyway."

And I also thought to myself, If they don't have the manners and decency to return a phone call it doesn't say much for their character.

It was an early indicator of the sort of problems I would face over the course of a season with Laois, and which, ultimately, led to my decision to step down from the post after just one year of what was to be a three-year term.

As a first foray into inter-county management, my year in charge of Laois was certainly an eye-opener. I was aware of the logistical demands of management at the highest level and was prepared for that. However, I entered an environment that I did not recognise and in which I felt there were greater forces at work that militated against my making a positive contribution.

My first connection with Laois came in September of 2011 when, in a surprise phone call, the Chairman of the county board, Brian Allen, asked me if I would be interested in talking to them about the vacancy created by the departure of the previous manager, Niall Rigney.

I was aware that they were also talking to other candidates but I was happy to meet them and discuss possibilities. When we did meet, I found Brian and his other officers to be welcoming, ambitious and positive. A few weeks later, they formally offered me the post and I accepted. Paul Fitzpatrick, who I had seen working with Sarsfields and who has vast experience as a fitness specialist, came on board with me.

Paul and I spent our journeys to and from various venues around Laois making plans, assessing our initial experiences with the players. It was clear from the start that there were difficulties, not least of which was the number of players who refused to wear the county colours. There were divisions in the county. Early on, it became obvious that the players did not trust the county board officers. They regarded them as football men. I was a county board appointment and that affected the judgement of some of the players.

Another division I noticed was between the clubs and the county: The club came first, the county came nowhere.

There were constant complaints about facilities. Some of those were justified. While a huge amount of work has gone into the development of O'Moore Park in Portlaoise, the facilities in other parts of the county are light years behind those I am accustomed to in Cork, Waterford and other counties I have visited.

I hope that doesn't offend some of the great people I met in Laois. We often trained in Clonad and you wouldn't find a more accommodating, welcoming bunch of people anywhere in Ireland. There were enthusiastic people like that in other parts of the county, too. I also found Brian Allen and his officers very helpful. Everyone wanted to do the right thing. The problem seems to be that everyone involved cannot come together and sort out whatever differences exist between them.

For a start, they should all ask why it is that they have had seven managers in ten years. They might also question why one of the best hurlers ever to play for Laois, Niall Rigney, left in frustration after two and a half years as manager.

They need a root and branch review of the whole environment in Laois. They need to strip the structures bare and start all over again, rebuilding relationships and setting a shared agenda.

The players also need to reassess their attitude. I wonder do they have dreams? I know some of them would love to win a Leinster Championship but I would question whether they know what is required to get to that level and if they are prepared to make the sort of commitment to the county cause that is required to be successful.

I found it frustrating. There is good work being done at under-age level. Both the minor and Under-21 teams went well in 2012. But I never felt that there was the same desire within the senior structures for everyone to work together for the one cause. There were constant battles, friction between players and officials.

A manager is judged on results. Ours were disappointing. It is hard for players to suffer some of the defeats that were inflicted on Laois in the Championship. I suffered as well. We lost to Dublin by 22 points. Limerick blasted six goals past us and we lost by 25 points. I needed time and I needed resources. Those resources included the players who would not play for the county. Laois cannot afford to be without seven players.

What county can?

From the start I knew I faced a huge challenge. It was part of the attraction of the job. Going in at the deep end didn't faze me. I was also encouraged by the warmth of the people I met in Laois, the county board officials, the players and members of clubs. Unfortunately, I also uncovered divisions within Laois. Until people find a way to resolve their differences, Laois will not be successful.

I became convinced they needed a manager from within the county who knows all the personalities intimately, who knows the history of what has happened in the county and who has a strong character. If they sort out the internal politics Laois can make progress.

They will do it without me. At the end of August 2012 I told the county board that there was no point in me continuing. It was time for us all to move on.

CHAPTER**18**

BACK TO THE FUTURE

Sometime in the future, I would like to draw on all the experiences I have enjoyed and endured as a player, a coach, and as a person, to manage the Cork senior hurling team.

I wouldn't call it an ambition, but if the opportunity presented itself then I would certainly go for it. It might never happen and I know that there are others who would similarly take the job and would be suitably qualified.

At the moment, the job could not be in better hands. If there is one man who can guide Cork hurling back from the precipice of despair and disunity to a position where we can compete again for All-Ireland titles, it is Jimmy Barry Murphy. I sincerely hope that he enjoys success, and soon.

Once you become involved in coaching you always want to test yourself. I have enjoyed the challenges of coaching within my own club and with other clubs in Cork and outside. My experiences have been mixed, but you have to see both sides, the good and the bad, in order to develop as a coach.

If the Cork job does not come my way I won't be disappointed. I have plenty of other avenues to explore and I will continue to get enjoyment from my involvement. The biggest kick I get from being involved is to see a team improve, to see players develop. That is why my involvement as a selector with the Sarsfields minor team in 2008 was one of the most enjoyable experiences of my life in hurling.

The club had won the Premier minor Championship in Cork in 2007. That was a very good team, which included my own son, Cian. But ten of them left the minor ranks at the end of that season, a huge turnover for any club. It meant that there weren't too many candidates willing to take over as team manager for 2008.

Dave O'Sullivan, whose sons, Conor and Eoin, are two outstanding players in the club, agreed to take the job. I met him in the bar after the AGM when he was appointed and told him I would give him any assistance he needed. He welcomed me on board and we brought Ray Ryan and Seanie Farrell in with us.

Dave worked really hard putting a team together and we worked alongside him. It was a struggle, but you could see as the months went by that the players were beginning to enjoy themselves more, and were coming together as a team. We kept on winning and reached the county final where we met Duhallow.

The seniors had already won the club's first county title since 1951 so you can imagine the atmosphere in the club. The boys responded brilliantly and we retained the title. It was a magnificent effort but, as much as winning the title, I enjoyed seeing the players improve individually and as a team.

•••••

Gaelic football doesn't particularly interest me at the moment. I will still go to see Glanmire and Cork play. I watch some of the big games on television. But if I missed one I wouldn't be too bothered.

There is no flair or imagination in the game any more. Tactics have taken over. Fortunately, tactics don't work in hurling. You can try something from time to time and you might get away with it but you cannot repeat it continually because the opposition will react to it.

Football is different. Managers can introduce tactics that stifle the opposition and therefore the game. They devise tactics that are designed to stop the opposition first. It is the same with football games all over the world; we see it in soccer, Australian Rules and American football.

Teams might contain players with artistry and flair but those players are not allowed to express themselves it if does not fit in with how the team manager wants his team to play.

This should not be interpreted as a criticism of the 2012 All-Ireland champions Donegal. I think they have been subjected to very unfair criticism in the last two years. People have not given Jimmy McGuinness and his players the credit they deserve for the way they have turned themselves from no-hopers into champions.

It was a gradual process and I admire McGuinness for what he did. The football they played in 2011 wasn't attractive but it was part of the process of creating a style, as well as building confidence. He had to change the mindset of a group of players and build their confidence through winning.

The players had the natural skills all the time. McGuinness didn't have to coach them to teach them how to catch the ball or kick the ball. He had to get them to commit, to dedicate themselves, to get the very best out of their ability. He had to convince them to buy into his philosophy of total commitment to Donegal, to make the sacrifices necessary to become physically fit and strong enough to compete and win at the highest level and to hone their skills. These were players who, prior to this, were clearly not giving the county jersey the respect it deserved. They weren't thinking like players who could win All-Ireland titles. McGuinness had to get into their heads, change those attitudes, and convince them that they must suffer physically and mentally in the pursuit of excellence.

His success was in making them believe and persuading them to make that commitment. He set the highest target. That was important. Some counties measure success too narrowly. They think winning a provincial title is enough, even getting through two rounds or enjoying a run in the qualifiers. Those are the counties who cannot win an All-Ireland title until they change those attitudes.

McGuinness also allowed his team to evolve. This year they began to play a more expansive game. They were more attractive to watch. They also took chances. That made them a more exciting team. They played to a plan that had been carefully worked out by the manager, but he also allowed them freedom of expression outside that plan.

There are some good coaches in football and there are some brilliant footballers around today. But they need assistance. The game has become bogged down by the negative tactics that kill skill and artistry.

One of the greatest skills in the game is fielding. I loved it. There was nothing better than getting as high as you could, using every muscle in your body to lift yourself into the air, and stretching high to pluck the ball above the outstretched arms of opponents.

The physical battle with an opponent like Jack O'Shea in the air was one of the great highlights of big Championship games. I had it every night I went training with Shea, Barry, Larry and Danny. He (Danny) used to drive me mad when he used his trick of unbalancing me with a nudge of his hip. He loved doing it. I loved trying to get the next ball.

It is a skill that needs to be rewarded. I would favour the introduction of a 'mark' when a player catches a ball cleanly from a dead ball situation such as a kick out, a line ball or a free kick. And I would insist that all line balls and all frees be taken from the ground.

Taking frees from the hand is destroying the game. There is no skill in it. Players are stealing yards without referees doing anything about it and they are making better angles for themselves when kicking for points.

The 'mark' would reward high fielding. It is a skill that is punished in the modern game. A player makes a big catch and comes down to be surrounded by players. More often than not he is blown for over-carrying.

I would also introduce a zone between the two 45s where a player is only allowed two solos before releasing the ball. It would have the effect of keeping the ball moving and would also help prevent mass defending. It is too easy to defend against a player who is soloing the ball too much.

One of the most obvious areas for improving football is the pick-up. Players should be allowed to pick the ball straight off the ground. There is no skill in touching the ball with your foot first and most players abuse it anyway.

Another skill that needs to be rewarded is long-range point scoring. You don't see it any more. I would favour introducing a zone between 35 and 45 metres from each goal. If you kick a point from outside that zone you should be rewarded with two points.

There was a time when the GAA was accused of being too slow to make changes. That is no longer the case. Radical changes have been made to the

GAA over the last 10 years. The rules of the games have been tinkered with to a considerable extent. Football now needs some modifications to make it more attractive for the paying customer and for the players. Physical fitness is very important but skill and rewarding skill should be the priority.

Hurling doesn't need rule changes. It needs a strong, competitive Cork team back competing with Kilkenny, Galway, Tipperary and the rest.

•••••

In the evenings from my home I can hear the excited shouts of the youngsters in the field. They call to me sometimes looking for hurleys. They are bright-eyed and enthusiastic, and sometimes full of mischief. They remind me of someone.

Glanmire has changed as Ireland has changed. Our setting is more tranquil now that the motorway has diverted cars and lorries away from the narrow road that winds through Sally Brook, Riverstown and Glanmire itself. The rivers, the woods and the scenery have attracted more people and the population has grown substantially.

It is a vibrant and busy place. I have never left. I am as happy here as I could be anywhere, making hurleys and taking pleasure from the fact that they are being used by players here in Glanmire, in Cork city and county, and in various places all over the country.

I still stroll down to Sarsfields a few days every week. It is where it all started for me and it is still a place in which I find comfort. We fought wars in those fields. We bled for the jersey, for our neighbours and our club. Good men looked after me, gave me guidance and encouragement.

My journey began here. It has taken me all over the world, to countries and continents I thought I would only experience through the covers of my history and geography books. With my attitude to school books that experience would have been very limited!

The road I have travelled has not always been smooth.

I have enjoyed great triumphs but I have also encountered despair. I have survived. I look at the kids chasing the small ball around the field and I hope they enjoy their sport as much as I have.

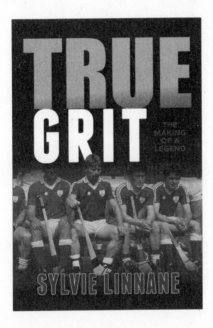

SYLVIE LINNANE is best remembered as the most courageous hurler to play Ireland's greatest game in modern times. For well over a decade, Sylvie was the iconic figure who personified Galway's epic struggle to become the nation's No.1 hurling team.

True Grit: The Making of a Legend recounts the story of the making of the boy, the making of the man and, ultimately, the making of the legend known throughout the country simply as 'Sylvie'.

Sylvie's unique autobiography is more than just an inspirational sports story. It's a vivid social and cultural history of a disappeared Ireland, and a tribute to a lost generation of Irishmen who left their homes and farms in search of a better life.

Sylvie Linnane played in seven All-Ireland finals in a glorious and memorable decade, when his heroic performances, deep in the Galway defence, earned three All-Ireland titles (1980, '87 and '88), two National League titles, five Railway Cups and three Oireachtas tournaments.

Now, the story of this three-time All Star award winner, is revealed in *True Grit: The Making of a Legend*.

ISBN: 978-0-9573954-4-2

Price: €15.99

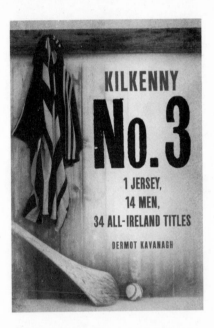

THE MOST precious territory in Kilkenny is the 75 square yards that front the county's goalposts. It is the heart of Kilkenny hurling and, down through time, it has always been the most safely guarded.

For more than a century of Kilkenny hurling, a princely total of 14 men have done everything asked of them – stretched every sinew, flexed every muscle, shed tears and often blood – to defend and protect that prized rectangular piece of ground.

In total, those 14 men have brought home to Kilkenny 34 All-Ireland senior titles. They are, indeed, men apart. From the light figure of Jack Rochford, the 5'7" Paddy Larkin, the 6'2" Pa Dillon, the burly Jim 'Link' Walsh, the tall and languid presence of Brian Cody, the granite-like 5'10" of Noel Hickey to the fleet-footed JJ Delaney, all of these men have handed the No.3 jersey down to one another with great pride and conviction.

This is the remarkable story of those 14 men and the story of how they safely brought home to Kilkenny an amazing 34 All-Ireland titles.

ISBN: 978-0-9573954-0-4
Price: €14.99

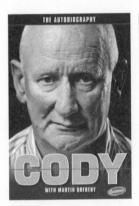